# DESERTS OF THE EARTH

For Elke and Gina

# DESERTS OF THE EARTH

## Extraordinary Images of Extreme Environments

Text and photographs by

### MICHAEL MARTIN

Foreword by

### MICHAEL ASHER

Specialist articles by

### PROFESSOR DR KLAUS GIESSNER

### DR ULRICH WERNERY

### PROFESSOR DR STEFAN DECH

with 271 colour illustrations

Thames & Hudson

# CONTENTS

# Foreword by Michael Asher

Once, sitting on a hillside in the Sinai Desert, alone but for my camel, I was startled by a swooshing sound like waves rolling to the shore. Looking up, I saw that the desert sky was black with flamingoes – thousands upon thousands of big birds, heading north. The seashore-sound was the whisper of their wings beating in harmony. For a moment I sat transfixed by the beauty of the sight. It was an instant that seemed to last for infinity, a split second of perfect union between myself and nature. I have often had such feelings in the desert – these lonely landscapes have given me some of the most profoundly spiritual experiences of my life.

The deserts of the Earth are places of vital importance to the human spirit. In an age of burgeoning cities and vast populations, they offer sanctuary to the imagination. Where else can one travel for a week, or even a month, without coming across a village, an asphalt road, or another person? To travel in the world's deserts is, even today, to enter a different dimension. Here, it is still possible to experience nature in its most primitive and unspoiled form. Here, one can still encounter qualities we have expelled from our technological world: solitude, silence, a link with the Earth, and with the cosmos that transcends time itself. The desert is a landscape of strange paradoxes. Standing

alone on a plain that stretches to every horizon, a human being is confronted with the reality of his own smallness. It is like being a speck on the shore of eternity, adrift in the incredible power and majesty of the universe. At the same time, the emptiness seems to magnify everything; the tracks of animals, grass, trees, stones, water, the relics of human activity come into precise focus. There are no crowds, no endlessly roaring engines, no works of man to stand between you and the planet. Everything you see, hear, smell and feel becomes laden with new meaning, as if you are experiencing it for the first time. To travel in the desert is to enter a new space-time continuum. In no other environment does the past lie so near to the present. Records of hundreds of thousands of years, of ice ages, earthquakes, droughts, torrential rains, of migrations of men and animals, are written on rocks and dunes, in cave paintings, and on the surface itself. In the Sahara it is possible to pick up stone tools used by Neolithic man, whose campfires lit the night here thousands of years ago.

Nowhere is nature's power more apparent than in the desert. All around, one can see features carved into forms – sometimes fantastic and surreal – by wind and water over millennia. On desert nights of perfect serenity, the sky seems heavy with stars. Yet this same still landscape can quickly erupt into terrifying motion. Roaring winds of breathtaking speed can race across the surface carrying vortices of dust hundreds of metres high. At these times, the Earth itself seems malevolent and alive.

Life everywhere in the desert seems a miracle. An oasis of palm trees is a haven in the emptiness. In the Empty Quarter of Arabia, the world's largest sand desert, there is a species of shrimp whose eggs can lie in the sand for decades waiting for the next shower of rain. Human societies that have adapted to this harsh terrain have often displayed the highest qualities to which we can aspire: courage, generosity, hospitality, loyalty and patience. These cultures have lessons for us. Many still experience a bond with the Earth and with creation that we city-dwellers have lost.

Never have these many aspects of the desert been captured so perfectly as in this book by Michael Martin – the only man ever to have crossed all the deserts of the Earth. In these images from his epic journey of five years and a hundred thousand kilometres, he evokes the beauty and variety of the world's deserts in a way unrivalled by any other photographer of his time. Traditionally, we have not valued deserts. They have been wastelands for us both physically and spiritually, only of worth for the exploitation of minerals, or as massive dumping grounds. If Michael Martin's work has a single message, it is to show us how wrong this concept is.

These panoramas – whether the dunes of the Takla Makan, the Gobi, the Atacama, or the Empty Quarter, the rolling plains of Australia's Red Centre, the buttes and mesas of Nevada, the stony wastes of the Sahara, the volcanic vastness of the Danakil – are priceless, because they bring us closer to the mystery of life at its most profound. Michael Martin's work demonstrates more vividly than perhaps ever before the true nature of experience in some of the most magnificent landscapes on Earth.

# Setting the Scene by Michael Martin

During the last five years, together with my friend Elke Wallner, I have spent 900 days travelling across the deserts of the Earth. It was six years ago that I decided to make deserts the subject of my next book, my next lecture tour and my next TV film, and even then I knew that I was letting myself in for a massive undertaking. A glance at the atlas will reveal that a third of the Earth's surface consists of deserts and semi-deserts. Furthermore, for a period of almost twenty years, I had been making expeditions through the deserts of Africa, and had got to know all the perils and hardships of such journeys. At least I was able to profit from my African experiences when it came to dealing with people, bureaucracy, breakdowns and other such problems, but in the deserts of Asia, Australia and America there were often very different obstacles.

It was my good fortune to get to know Elke Wallner shortly before I set out on this great journey. She was not only my travelling companion at every stage, but also acted as camerawoman in making the TV film of our adventures. We encountered many precarious situations, and indeed our mode of travel – two of us on a motorcycle with no accompanying vehicle – was a major risk in itself. Added to that was the fact that many deserts lie in dangerous or almost inaccessible regions. In countries like Afghanistan, Yemen, Turkmenistan and Chad, our personal safety was constantly in jeopardy. It was therefore with much relief and gratitude that we finally returned home safe and sound to Munich after our odyssey.

Although our journeys were often adventurous in the extreme, adventure was not the end we had in mind. The landscapes and cultures alone were far too fascinating to be treated merely as the setting for our own heroic deeds, and the natives of these often hostile regions are certainly far more deserving of applause than a couple of well-equipped European travellers. The knowledge passed on from one generation to another, profound respect for the environment, an inner strength, and a firm belief in a solid set of values – these are all essential tools that enable the people to survive. They have an aura and a confidence that often exceeds anything that we Europeans are used to, and I have nothing but the deepest respect and admiration for them.

It was also evident, however, that the lives of many of these desert people are undergoing radical changes: video recorders, new roads and political developments have had a profound effect on life in the tents and yurts of the nomads. It is not for us to make judgments on the fact that story-tellers are being replaced by TV sets, or traditional costumes are giving way to nylon shirts. What is far more important is that these desert people should be responsible for themselves and should be allowed to choose their own future paths without constraint from outside.

We found it immensely exciting to meet so many different kinds of people in so many different kinds of desert, and to experience not only the major differences but also the evident similarities. Thus we learned a variety of ways to ride a camel or put up a tent. All the nomads share an overriding concern for the needs of their animals. Another common feature was the hospitality and the human warmth that we encountered from Mauritania to Mongolia, from Australia to Bolivia, and from Mexico to Ethiopia.

Our adventures play no part in this book, for these are the subject matter of my lectures and of our TV film. The focal point here is the photographs and the geography of the deserts. As a geographer, I have taken this opportunity to write a text which I hope will follow the classic model of regional studies by describing geographical conditions in the deserts, as well as shedding light on the botany, biology and many other aspects of the subject. In addition there are special contributions from three experts in particular fields, together with eighteen detailed satellite maps to complement the text. However, despite the extensiveness of text and maps, this book is meant primarily as a photographic record. For me, photography is the best medium through which to document both landscapes and people. In this context, I see myself as neither a photojournalist nor an artist, for the pictures are simply my own very personal means of showing the geographical and social conditions engendered by the deserts. The original photos can be seen in my slide presentations and in exhibitions, as well as in magazines, calendars, postcards, posters and on the Internet.

But of all media, it is the book that is and has always been the most important to me. Properly printed on high-quality paper, the pictures create a very special effect, which is enhanced by the graphic design. To be both author and photographer of this book has given me a wonderful opportunity to match words and pictures in order to create a comprehensive image of the Earth's deserts. It is the quintessence of all my work so far, but at the same time it is a spur to go on exploring these endlessly fascinating regions.

GREAT
BASIN
DESERT

MOJAVE

SONORA

CHIHUAHUA
DESERT

ATACAMA

PATAGONIAN DESERT

# WHAT IS A DESERT?

It is no easy task to define a 'desert'. From the earliest geographers right through to the great explorers of the nineteenth and twentieth centuries, there have been countless attempts to describe and define the term. In French and English, the derivation is the Latin *desertum*, which means an abandoned place, and has nothing to do with aridity or lack of rain. But if emptiness were the only criterion, many types of landscape could qualify. Modern geographers tend to be a little more precise, with definitions such as: 'A desert is a region where, as a result of little or no rainfall, there is scant vegetation with considerable gaps between.'

For Théodore Monod (1902–2000), the great French geographer who specialized in the subject, deserts were 'regions where the climate causes aridity, where as a result of the lack of adequate moisture, plant growth is reduced, develops again in isolated patches, and disappears at the borders – and where accordingly, in place of the chemical changes in the rock, there is mechanical change'. Elsewhere, he writes: 'The arid regions of the Earth are those where, as a result of insufficient water supplies, plant cover and soil are present in too small a quantity to give effective protection to the rocks against the actions of the atmosphere.' Consequently, for Monod a desert must have the following characteristics: a step-by-step reduction in plant life, disruption of what is at best an episodic water supply, which is present only in small quantities and generally in enclosed basins, a tendency for any settlements to be concentrated in particular areas, and the appearance of unusual morphogenetic processes which produce characteristic forms (e.g. dunes).

For all this, the term 'desert' remains imprecise, for it encompasses landscapes that range from the completely bare Tanezrouft Plateau to the Kalahari with its many trees

Sand ripples in the Rub al-Khali.

and bushes. There is also a clear distinction between the American concept of a desert and the European one. For the Americans, the word is used for virtually any arid region, so long as it cannot be used for agriculture. No doubt this is because North American deserts are nothing like as arid as the Sahara, which is the model for the European concept.

Théodore Monod rightly bemoans the lack of a word that would describe those regions which are not deserts, but which are named as deserts both by cartographers and by ordinary people. On the other hand, however, I must say that during my journeys through the deserts of the Earth, I have come across countless areas that really are deserts but have not been named as such. Does anyone speak of the Ladakh Desert? And yet this region, on the leeward side of the Himalayas, gets less than 100 mm rainfall a year.

In this book, we shall try to cover the whole range of deserts, but we shall confine ourselves to those that are arid. Volcanic islands, for instance, will not be dealt with, because their barrenness is the result of impermeability and not of climate. Such areas are called edaphic.

No-one would seriously designate as deserts the mountainous regions in the more moderate climates of the world –

the lack of vegetation there is caused by cold and not by lack of rain – but it is not so easy to exclude the polar regions. Their deserts have two causes: a lack of heat and a lack of water. The latter can be gauged by the precipitation statistics: in northern Greenland, for instance, precipitation is sometimes below 50 mm a year, more than half of the Antarctic registers between 60 and 100 mm, and at the South Pole the annual average is between 20 and 50 mm. Evaporation is low, around 50 mm, and is therefore often less than the precipitation. This ratio is reversed in the Sahara, where potential evaporation exceeds precipitation by as much as a thousandfold. However, most people would count the arid regions of northern Greenland and the eastern Antarctic as polar and not desert, because their prime characteristic is that they are cold, and the lack of vegetation is not due solely to lack of rain.

The deserts and semi-deserts (i.e. semi-arid regions) of the Earth cover an area of 45–50 million square kilometres, which is 33–36 per cent of the land. This makes them the largest natural form of landscape in the world. In Africa, for example, 76.5 per cent of the land north of the Equator can be called desert or semi-desert. You will find detailed information about the individual continents (based on the work of the distinguished German geographer Klaus Giessner) at the beginning of each respective chapter. However, before the distribution and the causes of these deserts are dealt with, the various distinctions and divisions must be explained, and for this exercise there are several methodological approaches.

A climatologist will tell you that one basic feature of any desert is the lack of rain throughout the year and the high levels of temperature and evaporation; a botanist will classify a desert as a large expanse of land that contains no durable form of vegetation; a hydrographer will regard annual negative water supply and the formation of lakes with no outlet as important hydrological features of the desert landscape; a geomorphologist will seize on specific elements of the relief, and so on. It is little wonder, then, that the different experts often disagree on boundaries. At the same time, it has to be said, these boundaries are generally fairly close to one another, and there are more agreements than disagreements.

In the context of climate alone, and the delineation of arid zones, there is a long list of formulae to establish what constitutes aridity – ranging from the simple ratio of rainfall to evaporation, to extraordinarily complex equations. All of them, however, use the relationship between rainfall, temper-ature and/or evaporation to derive hydrothermal statistics that will establish the degree of aridity. For example, Vladimir Köppen's climatic classification – which categorizes climatic zones by letters, with deserts designated as 'BW' – defines the borders of aridity as where the annual rainfall is less than double the average annual temperature, provided the rainfall takes place in winter. If it takes place in summer, a corrective factor of 28 is added to the double temperature value, and if the rainfall is throughout the year the corrective factor is 14.

None of these procedures can disguise the fact that there has never been a global formula for aridity, and so there is as little consistency over what constitutes the boundaries of a desert as over the classification of deserts in general. Nevertheless, there are criteria that enable deserts to be divided into three groups: arid, semi-arid and hyper-arid. The most reliable of these is vegetation, because this is more depend-ent on climate than the geomorphological structures. One can also call on vegetation to distinguish between arid steppes, semi-desert, desert and extreme desert. Here, the following definitions may be applied: in an arid steppe or savanna, plants appear to be close together against the horizon, even if the vegetation in the foreground seems to be scattered.

This is in contrast to the desert steppes or semi-desert, where gaps remain. In a full desert, the vegetation no longer seems diffused but simply contracted, i.e. in small patches or in dips, thus giving rise to an impression of bareness. In an extreme desert, there is no vegetation at all.

Rather less complicated is the distinction between cold (moderate) and warm (subtropical) arid regions. Here Vladimir Köppen's borderline is a mean annual temperature of 18°C. Cold and warm regions often dovetail – for instance in the Namib, where there is a band of cold coastal desert, some 40 km wide, leading to a warm inland desert.

Aridity is a useful criterion in the definition of deserts, but when it comes to a more comprehensive spatial classification, it is geography that comes into its own. Once again, there are many different approaches, but in my view the most accurate is that of Théodore Monod. He distinguishes between the northern belt, the southern belt and the polar regions. To the northern belt he assigns the North American deserts and those along the Afro-Asian diagonal. Both of these subgroups contain warm and cold deserts. The southern belt contains the South American, southern African and Australian deserts.

In this book, however, for a clearer overview the deserts have been divided according to continents. Within these, the arid zones are subdivided into individual regions, which may contain one or several deserts. Frequently, the different causes of these deserts shall also be looked at in detail, but the main differences and the resultant types of desert are dealt with in the next chapter. The individual landscapes will be described in the chapters covering the various regions, but more general information on form and origin is given towards the end of the book.

South of the Kuiseb, a dry river, lie the dunes of the Namib. These star-dunes,

reaching up to a height of 300 m, are among the tallest in the world. Aerial photo taken from 250 m.

# TYPES OF DESERT AND THEIR CAUSES

A view from outer space will show that a high proportion of the Earth's land surface consists of deserts and semi-deserts. They seem to encompass the Earth in two belts – one northern, the other southern. Between 20° and 40° of latitude in the northern hemisphere lie the North American deserts and semi-deserts, the Sahara, the Arabian and the Central Asian deserts; in the southern hemisphere are those of Chile and Peru, Australia and southwest Africa. These two zones of aridity would be even more striking if climatic maps were to extend out into the oceans – then the deserts on the western sides of the continents would stretch for huge distances over the sea. The double belt of deserts around the Earth is not uninterrupted, and does not run parallel to the Equator. Instead, it falls within diagonals: in the northern hemisphere it runs from Mauritania to the Gobi, and in the southern lies the South American Arid Diagonal.

In this chapter we shall be looking at the climatic processes that cause aridity and thus create deserts. Once we have grasped the causes, it will be easier to understand the geographical distribution of these deserts. It often happens that several of the processes we are about to describe join together to reinforce the aridity, but there are also particular combinations of winds and pressures that may reduce it, for climatic conditions are far too complex to be confined to one simple model. The theory of atmospheric circulation that is so crucial to our understanding of the world's climate is itself immensely complicated and is not to be conceived one-dimensionally – it has to be seen in the context of three-dimensional space.

TROPICAL DESERTS  The tropics (Cancer and Capricorn) are the two degrees of latitude above which the sun stands directly overhead at the beginning of summer (21 June in the northern hemisphere, and 22 September in the southern). They are situated at 23.5° north and south and divide the tropics from the subtropics. However, even though the region encompassed is called 'the tropics', this does not mean that conditions themselves are what we know as 'tropical'. On the contrary, the predominant feature is aridity. For a long time, this was attributed exclusively to the trade winds, and it is only during the last few decades that climatologists have recognized the influence of the Tropical Easterly Jet Stream (TEJ) – a high-velocity air flow – on the aridity of the Sahara and the Arabian deserts. First, though, we shall take a look at the trade winds, which blow constantly across the tropical latitudes and have been well known since the earliest days of sailing ships. They are a tropical element in the general atmospheric circulation, and blow from the subtropical high-pressure cells to the Equatorial trough.

To explain global atmospheric circulation in detail here would take us too far away from our subject, but I should like to glance swiftly at one important factor that is relevant to the origin of tropical deserts: the so-called Hadley cell. Above the Equator rise warm, moisture-filled air masses, which then cool off and discharge their rain over the Equator itself. The air masses then move at a great height from the Equator to the two

tropics. Above them, at heights of 10–12 km, there is an accumulation of air, and because of the tropopause – an impenetrable boundary between the troposphere and the stratosphere – the original air masses are unable to rise; they increase the air pressure at ground level, and gradually sink down. As the air masses below the tropopause lose height, so the pressure rises, which in turn causes a dry adiabatic warming of these masses. The relative moisture of the air is reduced, and so condensation and cloud formation become impossible. The dry air masses then blow close to the surface of the Earth, as dry trade winds, and return into the Equatorial trough. The Coriolis effect, caused by the Earth's rotation, deflects the winds, so that in the northern hemisphere they blow from the northeast, and in the southern from the southeast. This inner trade wind movement is known as the Hadley circulation. The classic view is that these winds are responsible for the aridity of the tropics.

Of all the deserts on Earth, it is the tropical ones that cover the largest area, and they include large sections of the Old World arid belt, stretching from the Sahara across the Arabian peninsula to the Thar in India and on to China. In the southern hemisphere they include almost all of Australia, and the Namib, the Kalahari and the Karoo in southern Africa. The causes are therefore not to be found in the relief, but are directly connected to the global atmospheric circulation and its resultant climatic zones. This is why they are called zonal arid regions.

It has long been a well-known fact that aridity on the tropic of Cancer is far greater than that on the tropic of Capricorn. In the Sahara a yearly rainfall of 5–20 mm is set against potential yearly evaporation of 5,000–6,000 mm. In Australia the rainfall is greater – at least 100 mm a year – but potential evaporation is only 2,400 mm, while in the Kalahari there are 200–400 mm of rain as opposed to just 2,000 mm potential evaporation. The classical explanation for this phenomenon was the greater land mass in the northern hemisphere: the resultant continentality was said to cause the extreme temperatures and the highest of 'highs' above the Sahara. This, however, is incorrect, because the most powerful anticyclone lies over southern Tibet.

It used to be said that the Harmattan (the northeast African trade wind) was so dry because it blew over such wide expanses of land. However, aerial surveys have shown that currents over North Africa that have nothing to do with the trade wind are just as stable and dry in the summer. The greater continentality of the northern hemisphere certainly plays a part, but it does not provide an adequate explanation for the aridity.

In the 1960s, the German climatologist Hermann Flohn (1912–97) proved the effect of the Tropical Easterly Jet Stream in relation to the aridity of the Sahara and the Arabian deserts. The TEJ arises in summer from the falling pressure between the seasonal extreme anticyclone over Tibet and the Equatorial Indian Ocean. It is in the upper regions of the troposphere at a latitude of $12^\circ$–$14^\circ$ north, and blows from the western Pacific to the eastern Atlantic. The transverse circulation runs anti-clockwise from its source over Asia, and finishes running clockwise over the Sahara and Arabia. As this transverse circulation weakens, so the sinking tendency of the trade winds is reinforced, thus suppressing the tropical monsoons on the Equatorial side of the tropic of Cancer. The Sahara and the Arabian deserts thus owe their extreme aridity to the transverse circulation of the TEJ, and the summer anticyclone over Tibet.

RELIEF DESERTS  Relief deserts lie in the rain shadow of mountains. They are only to be found in zones where there are consistent winds that transport moist air masses. Generally, these are the westerlies between latitudes $40^\circ$ and $70^\circ$ north and south of the Equator.

Precipitation takes place on the windward side of the ridges, which generally run at right angles to the direction of the wind.

On the leeward side, the sinking and warming air masses break up the clouds and drastically reduce precipitation. Geographers describe this as the föhn effect, but it is also known locally by such names as Chinook (USA) or Zonda (Argentina).

One such relief desert is the Great Basin, on the leeward side of the Sierra Nevada and the Cascade range; another is the Mojave, with Death Valley, on the southern side of the Great Basin. The Chihuahua lies in the rain shadow of the Sierra Madre Occidental, and in South America the semi-deserts of Patagonia on the leeward side of the Andes are typical relief deserts.

The effects of meagre precipitation owing to mountain barriers are often exacerbated by a tropical situation. One example of this is in central Iran, where the high basins of the Great Kavir and the Lut are sheltered from moist air masses by the Zagros Mountains in the west and the Elburz in the north.

The combination of continentality and shelter is the principal cause of the Central Asian deserts, which lie in basins that are surrounded by high mountain ranges. The extreme relief of the Himalayas also prevents the Indian monsoon from crossing the Tibetan Plateau into Central Asia.

CONTINENTAL INLAND DESERTS  Many relief deserts would receive adequate rainfall were it not for the mountain barrier, but in the centre of great land masses there are also arid regions which, even without these barriers, would still not receive the moist air. This applies especially to Asia, where between latitudes $35^\circ$ and $50^\circ$ north in particular there are vast arid areas stretching right across the continent. The aridity of the central and eastern parts of the Sahara is also reinforced by continentality. The effects of depressions coming from the Atlantic become weaker and weaker as they head eastwards, and the air masses lose their moisture, so that by the time they reach the regions that are far away from the sea, they have dried out. Thus geographical situation alone can lead to aridity. Continentality brings huge differences in temperature: in the deserts of Central Asia temperatures can range from $40^\circ$C below zero to $50^\circ$C above zero.

COASTAL DESERTS  Coastal deserts are one of the strangest types. The cliché of the hot, dry expanse of sand simply does not apply here. They are practically without rainfall, but are nevertheless relatively moist and cool. Examples are parts of the Sonora on the peninsula of Baja California, the Atacama in South America, and the Namib in southwest Africa. The aridity of these deserts is caused by their proximity to cold ocean currents that run parallel to the coast, i.e. the California current that comes from the north and runs along the Pacific coastline, the Humboldt current that runs from the Antarctic along the Pacific coast of South America, and the Benguela current – also from the Antarctic – that moves parallel to the Atlantic coastline of South Africa. The cold Canaries current contributes to the aridity of the coastal western Sahara, though here – in contrast to real coastal deserts – aridity increases further inland. In western Australia the aridity is also increased by a cold ocean current. It is striking that all these coastal deserts are situated on the western side of their continents, and the reason becomes clear if one takes a closer look at the cause.

On the western coasts of America and Africa, the surface water of the ocean currents is deflected seawards, so that land-wards the cold deep waters well up, and this further reduces the surface temperature of the already cold ocean current. The surface temperature of the Benguela current is between $12^{0}$C in winter and $17^{0}$C in summer. Off the coast of northern Chile, the water temperature is $10^{0}$C lower than normal at this latitude, on account of the Humboldt current, and off Peru it is $12^{0}$C lower. The cold surface of the sea also leads to a sinking of the air masses, which become cooler through contact with the surface. This results in an inversion layer which, for instance,

from 700 m to 1,700 m above the Benguela current causes the temperature to increase from $4^{0}$C to $9^{0}$C from bottom to top. There is a similar inversion over the Humboldt current, where from 600 m to 900 m the vertical rise in temperature is from $7^{0}$C to $11^{0}$C. The cooling air condenses and forms banks of fog, which normally lie offshore but can be driven inland by the wind. Then, however, the high temperature of the ground on the mainland causes turbulence which generally disperses the fog very quickly. When the air masses rise again, the inversion layer prevents condensation and therefore also precipitation in the form of rain.

SYRIAN DESERT   GREAT NAFUD   RUB AL-KHALI   NEGEV   GREAT KAVIR   LUT   KARA-KUM   KYZYL-KUM   THAR   SIND

DZUNGARIA   SINKIANG   GOBI   BEI SHAN   ALA SHAN   ORDOS   QAIDAM   TIBET

# THE DESERTS OF ASIA

NEGEV

SYRIAN
DESERT

GREAT
NAFUD

RUB AL-KHALI

USTYURT
PLATEAU

KYZYL-KUM

KARA-KUM

GREAT
KAVIR

LUT

BALUCHISTAN

SIND

THAR

BET-PAK-DALA
MYJUMKUM

SARY-
ISHIKOTRAU

DZUNGARIA

GOBI

BEI SHAN

ALA SHAN

ORDOS

SINKIANG

QAIDAM

TIBET

# OVERVIEW OF ASIA

Asia is the largest of the continents, covering an area of 15.7 million square kilometres, and it has the second largest area of deserts and semi-deserts. Thirty-seven per cent of the continent comes under this category, which proportionately is some way behind Africa and Australia, and in fact only three per cent counts as hyper-arid. Asia is not only vast, but also astonishingly varied in its landscapes and climate. The arid areas extend from the Sinai peninsula in the west to the desert steppes of the Gobi desert in the east, so that it is often difficult to delineate them.

In the following account, I have adhered to the general principles of division that govern this book, and have classified the deserts of Asia according to regions: thus the Rub al-Khali and the Great Nafud belong to Arabia, while the deserts of Iran and Afghanistan include the Great Kavir, the Lut and the Afghan desert regions. North and northwest from here are the deserts of what I have called Central Asia (west), including the Kara-Kum and the Kyzyl-Kum. The area to the northwest of the Indian sub-continent also has a large arid expanse, the eastern section of which is known as the Thar. As for the many deserts in China and Mongolia, the best known of which is the Gobi, I have called their location Central Asia (east). The district of Ladakh, which in terms of climate and culture belongs to Tibet, is also placed under this heading, even though it is actually part of India. The deserts of Asia originated from a variety of causes, and their location also varies from the tropics to the rain shadows on the leeward side of mountains and to vast interior land masses. Coastal deserts, caused by cold currents, are not to be found in Asia, where many of the deserts are part of the Old World arid belt that begins in the west with the Sahara, stretches out over the Arabian peninsula, across Iran and Afghanistan, and into Central Asia.

Scale: 1 cm = 350 km

# THE DESERTS OF ARABIA

Geologically, the Arabian peninsula is part of the old African land mass, though separated from this up as far as the Gulf of Suez by the rift valley of the Red Sea. It is 2,700 km long, 1,400–2,400 km wide, and covers an area of 3.5 million square kilometres. In terms of climate, the deserts of Arabia – like the Sahara – are typically tropical, though they are in the trade wind regions. The north is subject to winter rain and is influenced by the Mediterranean, while in the south the Omani Dhofar is in the monsoon area. The mountainous regions of Oman, Yemen and southwest Saudi Arabia have no desert country at all. In the north, the border between desert and steppe runs from Gaza north of the Dead Sea, then along the Jordanian Plateau to the Euphrates southeast of Aleppo. From there it goes southeast, reaches the Tigris at Tikrit, and runs via Baghdad at the foot of the Zagros Mountains all the way to the Persian Gulf. While the Great Nafud in the north and the Rub al-Khali in the southeast are clearly delineated by their basin structures, the names and borders of many other Arabian deserts often seem to be quite arbitrary. For instance, the most northerly desert regions have a variety of local names, which many maps lump together as 'Syrian Desert'.

The Sinai peninsula, however, is clearly defined: enclosed by the Red Sea – or, to be more precise, by the Gulf of Suez and the Gulf of Aqaba – it can be divided into north Sinai, the El Tih Desert and the south Sinai Mountains. The El Tih Plateau, with a yearly rainfall of 20–50 mm, is one of the most inhospitable areas of the peninsula. Living and economic conditions are far better in the mountainous region of south Sinai, where the yearly rainfall is 150–200 mm, which provides the nomads with good pasture in the wadis and on the slopes.

The Negev desert is a continuation of the Sinai deserts. With an area of 12,000 km², it covers sixty per cent of Israeli territory,

Dunes in the Rub al-Khali.

Mediterranean

Aleppo

SYRIA

Palmyra

SYRIAN
DESERT

Euphrates

Tigris

Tikrit

Baghdad

Zagros Mountains

ISRAEL

Jerusalem
Gaza

JORDAN

NEGEV

EL TIH
Sinai

Aqaba

IRAQ

GREAT
NAFUD

KUWAIT

Persian Gulf

Red Sea

TIHAMA

SAUDI
ARABIA

Riyadh

BAHRAIN

QATAR

Dubai

UAE

Muscat

RAMLAT
AL WAHIBA

RUB AL-KHALI

Ras ar Ruways

OMAN

YEMEN

Dhofar

Thulla

Hadhramaut

Sanaa

Indian
Ocean

and is divided into the partly loess-covered (loess is a a deposit of wind-blown sediment) north and the mountainous central and southern Negev. The transformation of parts of this desert into an area of intensive farming counts as one of the greatest achievements of Israel's agrarian technology.

Seventy-one per cent of the Arabian peninsula belongs to Saudi Arabia. A glance at a climate chart of Saudi Arabia will reveal a striking contrast between the highlands and mountains in the west and the deserts inland and along the coast. The Red Sea marks the natural boundary between Saudi Arabia and its neighbours: between the coast and the mountains to the east, the coastal desert of Tihama reaches as far as Yemen. The climate here is sultry, with less than 100 mm of rain a year. East of this narrow coastal strip rises the steep range of mountains on the western border, which forms the edge of the rift valley. Here the climate is semi-arid, with moderate temperatures, though these vary considerably according to the seasons. The rift valley mountains are joined in the east by the inland highlands, which are predominantly rocky desert with no sand dunes at all. Further to the east is the central Arabian cuesta, with its sequence of steep ridges and gentle slopes.

In the southeast is the desert that has fired the imagination of many an explorer: the Rub al-Khali, or 'Empty Quarter'. First crossed in 1930–31 by the Englishman Bertram Thomas, it still ranks as one of the most inaccessible regions in the world. It lies in a geological basin, and extends into Yemen and Oman. With an area of 780,000 km², it is the biggest of all sand deserts, and its dunes – reaching up to 300 m in height – stretch for more than 500 km from north to south, and over 1,300 km from east to west. Large areas of the Rub al-Khali are completely without water and vegetation, and only in the northeast are there a few springs. The yearly rainfall in this hot, dry region is well under 50 mm.

The smaller counterpart in the north is the Great Nafud. This too lies in a basin with very clear boundaries, and it covers an area of 78,000 km². As with the Rub al-Khali, its surface consists of very uneven dunes. There is no surface water, and the occasional rainfall brought in by the winter cyclones from the Mediterranean regions quickly seeps away into the sand.

The coastal deserts of the Arabian-Persian Gulf and the gravel surfaces of the Dibdibah are what form the Gulf Region. It is to this part of the Arabian peninsula that the bordering states owe their economic prosperity, because the structure of the underground rock strata has given rise to a sequence of

Scale: 1 cm = 125 km

A member of the ruling family of Dubai, hunting with a gyrfalcon.

impermeable folds that make ideal 'traps' for oil. The most important oil-bearing rocks lie at a depth of between 1,500 3,000 m, and they have been opened up into countless oilfields. The Gulf Region contains the richest oil reserves in the world, and nowhere can oil and natural gas be produced more quickly or more cheaply than in the Arabian peninsula.

Oil production has been in operation in Bahrain since 1934 and in Saudi Arabia since 1938. Traditional Bedouin societies then swiftly turned into modern states, which looked on the Bedouins themselves as an anachronism and a possible threat to security. Nevertheless, when the allocation of funds and official positions comes on the agenda, a person's social status (his or her origins, and rank within that community) remains an important factor.

Cattle farming, in the few places where it is still to be found, is in the hands of foreigners. It depends on dry feed and alfalfa, which is produced at great expense on irrigated land. In these oil-rich countries, the breeding of dromedaries has now become little more than a hobby. People live in comfortable, air-conditioned houses, and it is only on special occasions that families may stay in canvas tents, though these too will be equipped with all modern comforts.

These oil-producing states have had a reasonable amount of success in diversifying their economies. Energy and capital are available in abundance, but generally expertise, labour and even raw materials have to be imported. Saudi Arabia in particular has gone in for agriculture on a large scale, and produces considerably more wheat than is needed for home consumption.

Saline soil, groundwater lowering – because of excessive extraction – and sand drifts are only a few of the problems faced by this large-scale farming. In addition, production costs are often so high that it is cheaper to import.

The smaller Gulf States of Bahrain, Kuwait, Qatar and the United Arab Emirates are banking on their function as trading and financial centres to reduce their dependence on oil and gas exports. The UAE have led the way in marketing their desert as a tourist attraction.

The Rub al-Khali or 'Empty Quarter' is the largest, most arid desert in Arabia. The endless expanse and the 300 m high dunes make it one of the most inaccessible of the world's deserts.

Bedouins from Ramlat al Wahiba meet with fishermen at Ras ar Ruways on the Omani coast. The fish, which are caught in nets, are transported in cross-country vehicles across the desert to the capital, Muscat.

On a morning during Ramadan, very few people are around in the alleyways of Thulla, a town in Yemen.

In Sanaa, only the minarets reach higher than the tall,

richly decorated houses of the Old City.

Young people in Yemen.

Sanaa is one of the few places in Arabia to have
retained its medieval appearance. In the Old City
there are some 6,000 houses, generally four to six
storeys high with walls half a metre thick.

Rich young men test their cars out along the strand in Dubai.

# THE DESERTS OF IRAN AND AFGHANISTAN

The Iranian highlands lie in the middle of the Old World arid belt, where the subtropical trade winds blow, and they extend far into Afghanistan. While the Iranian deserts of Great Kavir and Lut have been thoroughly researched, there has been little exploration of the Afghan desert regions of Baluchistan and Registan because of the political instability of the area in recent times.

The Great Kavir and the Lut lie in two high basins that are sheltered from moist air masses by the Zagros Mountains in the west and the Elburz Mountains in the north; they are separated by the area around Tabas. The Great Kavir, marked on many maps under its Persian name of Dasht-e-Kavir, is a salt desert and one of the most barren, lifeless regions in the world. There is no place here for man or beast, and so there are no settlements of any kind. The Lut covers an area of 166,000 km² and, like the Kavir, consists of a series of partial basins. Two landscapes that are characteristic of the Lut are kalut and yardang.

The former refers to parallel ridges, up to 80 m high, which are separated by narrow corridors and are created by the north-northwesterly winds and corrosion. Yardangs are linear ridges of rock that are rounded upwind and sharply crested downwind. The kaluts stretch out in lines across the surface of the desert, and the expanses of yardangs are called Shar Lut, or desert towns.

In contrast to the southwest Lut, whose face is pitted with erosion, the southeast has been built up with massive deposits that can create dunes up to 200 m high. Potential evaporation in the Lut is 5,000 mm a year, and the annual rainfall is less than 50 mm. In summer, the temperature rises to 50°C, which makes it one of the hottest and driest deserts on Earth, with many areas virtually abiotic. There are not even any signs of earlier life, such as subfossil shells or fossilized diatoms, and – unlike the Sahara – nor are there any signs of earlier human settlements.

A nomad from central Afghanistan.

Elburz Mountains

Tehran

GREAT KAVIR

IRAN

Zagros Mountains

Persian Gulf

Kerman

LUT

Bam

Pamir

Mazar-e Sharif

Hindu Kush

Herat

Band i Amir

Kabul

AFGHANISTAN

Kandahar

DASHT-MARGO

Helmand

REGISTAN

PAKISTAN

BALUCHISTAN

Arabian Sea

Asia
IRAN AND AFGHANISTAN

Even today, the Lut is a huge barrier to traffic between the southeast of Iran and the rest of the country.

In the summer months, the nomadic tribes of Iran live in the mountains south of the Lut. Inside their spacious tents are the huge looms on which Persian carpets are made, which are so beloved of Europeans. Shortly before the onset of winter, the goats, tents and household goods are packed onto lorries, and everyone moves camp to the mountains of the Persian Gulf.

On the edges of the Lut and Kavir basins, there are oases. They owe their existence to qanats. This technique supplies the oases with groundwater from the mountains, and was developed centuries ago in Iran and later found its way to China. Qanats are horizontal springs which tap the groundwater at the foot of a mountain, and use the natural slope to direct it to the surface. The tunnels that carry the groundwater are linked to the surface by means of numerous vertical shafts. These qanats can be as much as 70 km long, while the tunnels may be up to 400 m below the surface. While modern deep wells use up supplies of fossil groundwater, which can never be replenished, qanats only use groundwater that comes from rainfall in the mountains, which makes it doubly sad that this method of water extraction is very much on the wane, both in Iran and elsewhere.

The Iranian highlands – extending far into Afghanistan – incorporate the desert regions of southern Afghanistan, which are divided up into east and west by the River Helmand. To the east is Registan, a sandy region that covers 25,000 km$^2$ and provides important additional pasture land for the Baluchis living in the Helmand Valley. But there are no permanent settlements in this desert, and the only shade is that given by the saxaul trees. The local name for the desert regions west of the Helmand is Dasht-Margo. The surface here consists predominantly of gravel, but there are also strata of salt clay deeper down, and expanses of sand in the form of shifting dunes.

The Afghan section of the Iranian highlands contains the Asiatic fold mountains that begin in northeast Afghanistan with the Pamirs, and continue across the Hindu Kush to the ranges in central Afghanistan, which fork west and southwest. Although the rainfall is considerably higher here than in Registan or Baluchistan, there are also desert conditions here, especially in the rain shadows of the mountains. In the summer months, the heights offer refuge to the nomads – during the winter, reserves of water are created by the snow, which last through the summer. In the cold winter months, however, the nomads retreat to the northern and southern plains of Afghanistan.

Scale: 1 cm = 100 km

53

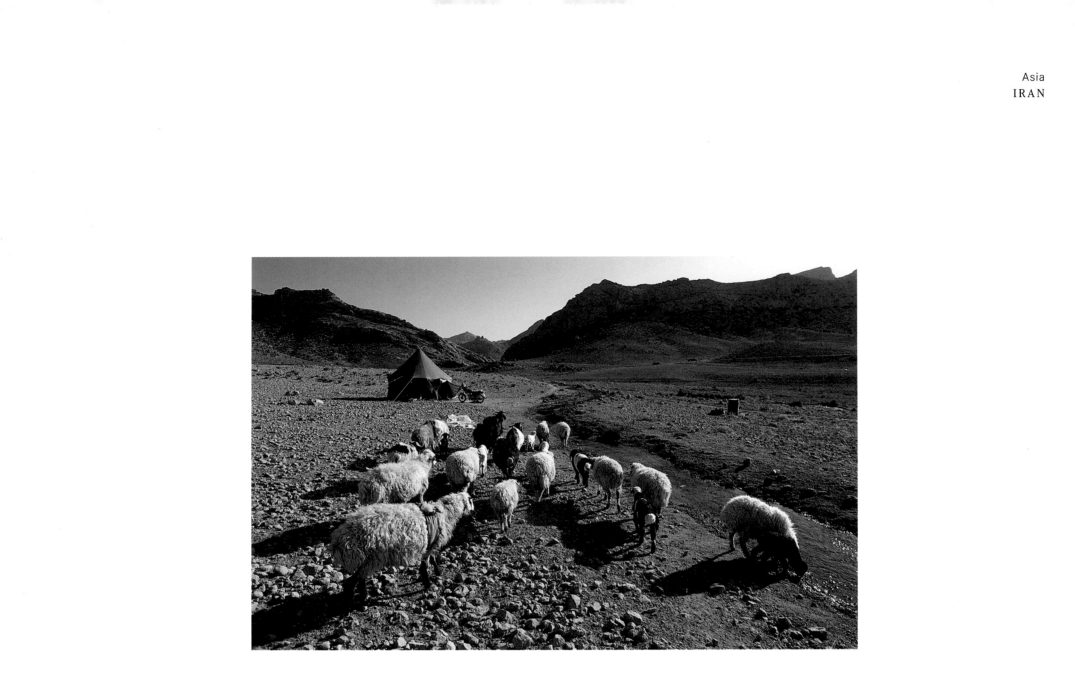

Summer in Iran, and the Qashqai nomads pitch camp in the mountains west of Bam.

Iranian nomads painstakingly weave large carpets in their tents.

It can take several women many months to create a single carpet.

Girl in an Iranian school for nomads.

Scenes of Afghanistan.

The seven shining lakes of Band-i-Amir, with their varying shades of blue, lie in giant steps within the mountainous desert of Afghanistan. They are linked by waterfalls.

It takes two hours to walk through the dark, partly destroyed Salang Tunnel,

which links Kabul with northern Afghanistan.

High passes make for slow traffic in central
Afghanistan. Early in the morning, the owner
of a teahouse waits for the first lorry drivers.

# THE DESERTS OF CENTRAL ASIA (WEST)

The Central Asian deserts lie in a huge basin that was formed more than sixty million years ago, when the mountain ranges of the Himalayas, Tien Shan and Pamir enclosed the existing sea and transformed it into a continental lake. During the next twenty-five million years India and Asia continued to merge together, and thus the basin was raised up like a wedge by the land mass of India and emptied out to the west into what is now the Black Sea and the Mediterranean. In Central Asia little remained of the inland sea, other than the Caspian and Aral seas.

The fact that this mighty basin is now so far from the ocean means that there is very little rainfall there, to the extent that the land between the Caspian Sea in the west and the Altai in the east consists of deserts, semi-deserts and steppes. What they all have in common is that they are largely covered in sand, with more or less dense vegetation. High dunes do not exist here – the sand stretches out in waves that are similar to the dead dunes of the Sahel region in Africa. The most familiar shrub in these Central Asian dry regions is the saxaul.

Russian geographers divide these Central Asian arid regions into northern and southern types, according to their climate. The northern type includes the Ustyurt Plateau in southern Kazakhstan, the Bet-Pak-Dala Steppe (Hunger Steppe), the Myjumkum semi-desert, and the Sary-Ishikotrau sand region south of Lake Balkhash.

The low rainfall is evenly distributed throughout the year; summers are hot, winters cold, and the average temperature over the year is below 10°C. Where the average annual rainfall is between 200 and 300 mm, grassland tends to dominate, but where it is below this figure the steppes become semi-deserts. The rainfall never goes below 150 mm, however.

The southern type of Central Asian arid region includes the Kara-Kum and Kyzyl-Kum deserts, and the Golodnaya Steppe.

A camel herdsman in the Kara-Kum desert.

KAZAKHSTAN

Lake Balkhash

Aral Sea

BET-PAK-DALA

SARY-
ISHIKOTRAU

USTYURT
PLATEAU

Caspian
Sea

Syr-Darya

MYJUMKUM

KYZYL-KUM

Almaty

UZBEKISTAN

Tien Shan

GOLOD-
NAYA

TURKMENISTAN

KARA-KUM

Samarkand

Amu-Darya

Ashgabat

Merv

Here the rain falls mainly in winter and spring, the summers are dry and very hot, but the winters are not especially cold. The average annual temperature is between 13°C and 18°C, which is considerably higher than that in the north. Here the aridity is nothing like as intense as in the Sahara, and so the dunes of Kara-Kum and Kyzyl-Kum are covered with grass and shrubs.

The Kyzyl-Kum desert lies between the rivers Amu-Darya and Syr-Darya in what is now Uzbekistan, and with an area of 200,000 km² is much smaller than the Kara-Kum. The landscape, however, is more varied, as many of the mountainous regions were once islands in the Central Asian inland sea. On many of the plateaux in the foothills, sand is mixed with gravel, and the plains are full of the red sand from which the Kyzyl-Kum takes its name (kyzyl means red, and kum means sand).

The Kara-Kum desert lies west of the Amu-Darya in present-day Turkmenistan, and it covers an area of 490,000 km², reaching as far as the Caspian Sea. Large areas of the Kara-Kum desert are covered with sand, but this is not black, despite the name (for kara means black). In Turkoman the word 'Kara-Kum' is only used for those parts of the desert that contain grass. This distinguishes them from the akkum or white sand, where there is no grass. It may well be, then, that the word kara actually means

fertile, as in the geographical expression for 'black earth' (which is chernozem).

The Amu-Darya and its branches have always been vitally important for the people in the Kara-Kum and Kyzyl-Kum deserts. Ancient history gives it the name of Arax or Oxus, and it is described as a river of gigantic proportions. Its source is in the Hindu Kush, and once it fed no less than 20,000 springs on its course to the Aral Sea, which was once the fourth biggest lake in the world. In 1960, it still covered an area of 70,000 km², and there were some 60,000 people employed in the fishing industry. Under the Soviet Union, however, the region was used to cultivate cotton, and the river water was diverted to irrigate the cotton fields. The consequences for the Aral Sea were catastrophic. Between 1960 and 1990, the volume of water dwindled by more than fifty per cent, while the saline content increased sixfold. Today the volume of water is only a fifth of what it used to be, the fishing industry is defunct, and chemical waste dumped on the former islands of the Aral Sea has polluted the air, water and soil. The people of the Uzbek province of Karakalpakstan have an average life expectancy of forty years, and the high infant mortality rate and incidence of congenital deformities provide further evidence of this disaster.

Scale: 1 cm = 125 km

The collective farms of the former Soviet Union today house livestock farmers from Turkmenistan and Kazakhstan.

The herds of animals now belong to them.

Samarkand, on the southern edge of the Kyzyl-Kum desert,

is one of the most famous trading places on the Silk Road.

A crater in the centre of the Kara-Kum desert in
Turkmenistan, where natural gas has been
burning for decades.

# THE DESERTS OF THE INDIAN SUBCONTINENT

In the northwest of the Indian subcontinent lies a huge arid zone that takes in large areas of Rajasthan west of the Aravalli Mountains, and reaches across the India-Pakistan border as far as the Indus. Although rainfall is never less that 150 mm a year, and there are practically no regions without vegetation, man has contributed largely to the creation of deserts here.

The biggest of these is the sand desert of Thar, which extends as far as Pakistan: the northern part is called Cholistan, and the southern Nara. The Jhelum, a tributary of the Indus, and the Indus itself enclose the Thar desert, which is mainly in Pakistan and is also known as the Sind-Sagar-Doab. A second desert, the Sind, is situated in the Pakistan province of that name, on the Lower Indus. The whole region forms part of the Indo-Iranian arid region, which extends west of the Indus through Baluchistan and into Iran. The effects of the Equatorial monsoon reach as far as the Sulaiman and Kirthar ranges that form the border of Baluchistan towards the Indus plain. Dry winters and a lack of rain during the summer monsoons are typical of these regions east of the mountains. Baluchistan, on the other hand, has a dry, subtropical desert climate with rainfall in the winter months.

The sandy desert of Thar has no oases owing to the shortage and general inaccessibility of groundwater. Although the region west of Jaisalmer is almost completely covered with dunes that have a thin layer of vegetation, only about half of Cholistan – a section of the Thar that is in Pakistan – is sandy desert.

Most of the literature on the Thar desert tends to describe it as man-made. Today, most experts would say that this is misleading and that the principal causes of desertification are climatic, but there is still no denying the significant influence of human activity on the ecology of this region. Deforestation – the wood used for burning and building – and the destruction of

Early morning in the Thar desert.

Chagai Hills

BALUCHISTAN

Makran Mountains

PAKISTAN

Sulaiman Mountains

THAL DESERT

Jhelum

Punjab

CHOLISTAN

NARA

Indus

Kirthar Mountains

SIND

• Karachi

Jaisalmer

T H A R

• Pushkar

Delhi

Aravalli Range

Arabian
Sea

INDIA

Indian
Ocean

grassy areas through overgrazing have caused problems: the summer rain no longer penetrates the soil but runs off the surface, which further reduces the level of groundwater. The completion of the Rajasthan Canal in 1986, which carries water from the Punjab and, together with subsidiary canals, distributes it over a system that covers more than 3,500 km, has brought about a tenfold increase in the population of the area that is served. The Thar today is the most densely populated and most cultivated desert in the world.

The problem of an ever-increasing population that makes competing demands on an ever-shrinking area of land is clear to see in Cholistan. In former times, the peasants used to rear cattle there. But as the irrigated land of the Punjab pushed ever further south, thereby turning pasture into arable land, the herdsmen were forced to take their cattle further afield. They ended up leading a nomadic existence, and so with their gigantic herds contributed to the large-scale desertification of Cholistan quite involuntarily.

Although the western border of the Indian subcontinent is formed by the Indus plain, we might take a quick look at Baluchistan, since most of it lies in Pakistan. Ladakh, however, on the other side of the main ridge of the Himalayas, belongs both geologically and culturally to Tibet, and should therefore be classified as a Central Asian desert.

West of the Sulaiman and Kirthar Mountains lies the broad expanse of the Baluchistan Plateau, which extends into Iran in the west. Geologically, it also counts as part of the Iranian highlands. To the north, towards Afghanistan, the borders are formed by the Chagai and Toba Kakar Mountains, and bare mountain ranges run right through this region. The driest areas are in the northwest, but the central Makran Mountains also offer very little to sustain life. In Baluchistan there are five million Baluchi, divided up into a number of rival groups that spend the summer with their cattle, living as nomads in the mountain pastures, and then go down into the valleys of the Indus for the winter.

In Rajasthan, on the Indian border with
Pakistan, women fetch water from the wells
and carry it in pots back to their village.

Rajasthanis are good judges of camels, which are still the most important animals

for work and transport in the Thar desert.

The camel market at Pushkar takes place during the weeks that precede the full moon in the holy month of Kartik Purnima.

All the desert people of Rajasthan go there with their camels.

On the edge of the Pushkar camel market,

a boy quenches his thirst at a drinking trough

after a hot day.

There are fifty-two ghats leading down to the holy lake of Pushkar on the edge of the Thar desert.

Pilgrims take a ritual bath on the steps of the ghats.

A Rajasthani watches his son milking the camels in the evening sun.

The milk goes into copper churns.

# THE DESERTS OF CENTRAL ASIA (EAST)

The eastern deserts of Central Asia are in the northwest of China and the south of Mongolia. Most of these are basins that are surrounded by high mountain ridges. Their aridity is primarily due to two factors: their distance from the sea, and the fact that they are sheltered by the surrounding mountains. The cyclones (areas of low pressure) caused by the westerlies have scarcely any influence here because the Atlantic is so far away, and from the east the moisture content of the Chinese monsoon is quickly dissipated. Another cause of aridity is the proximity of these deserts to the cold winters of Siberia, whose sinking – and so very dry – air masses come in from the north and block the westerly winds.

A typical feature of these Central Asian deserts is their continental climate, with extreme temperatures in summer and winter. The lack of clouds in summer leads to intense heat, e.g. in the Turpan Depression, where temperatures may rise as high as 50°C, whereas in winter they fall as low as minus 25°C, and in Mongolia to below minus 40°C.

French scientist Théodore Monod and the Russian Michail P. Petrov divide the deserts of Central Asia into the Dzungaria, Sinkiang, Gobi, Bei Shan, Ala Shan, Ordos, Qaidam and Tibet.

DZUNGARIA    The Dzungaria is a valley between the Altai Mountains in the north and the Tien Shan Mountains in the south. On its lower levels the contours are more or less even, with a preponderance of reg (small stones), salt and clay. The only variation is the areas with dunes. There is very little vegetation in the centre, but on the fringes forests and meadows on the mountain slopes provide a stark contrast.

SINKIANG    The Sinkiang is much more typical of desert country. Monod and Petrov are not referring here to the autonomous province of Sinkiang, but to the desert region between the Tien Shan, Pamir, Kunlun and Bei Shan Mountains,

Altai

Ulan Bator

MONGOLIA

DZUNGARIA

GOBI

Tien Shan

Urumqi

CHINA

Turpan

TURPAN DEPRESSION

Korla

BEI SHAN

ALA SHAN

Tarim Basin

Lop Nor

Hohot

Kashgar

SINKIANG

Dunhuang

ORDOS

Peking

TAKLA MAKAN

Hotan

QAIDAM

Koko Nur

Yellow River

Pamir Kunlun

CHANG TANG
DESERT

Ladakh Kailash

TIBET

Himalayas

which covers an area of 700,000 km². The dominant geological structure is the Tarim Basin, most of which is covered by the dunes of the Takla Makan (320,000 km²). These made the Takla Makan virtually inaccessible for a long time, and the caravans of the Silk Road used to skirt this desert. In 1895, the Swedish explorer Sven Hedin barely escaped with his life when trying to cross the Takla Makan. Today, however, it is crossed by a tarred road which has opened up its rich oilfields. Even the legendary Lop Nor, in the east of Takla Makan, into which the Tarim once flowed and which was made famous by Sven Hedin's book *The Wandering Lake*, is now relatively easy to reach.

Oases such as Hotan, Kashgar and Aksu are situated on the edge of the Tarim Basin, where the meltwater from the Pamir, Kunlun and Tien Shan Mountains provides them with all the water they need. This also applies to the Turpan Oasis, even with its extreme summer temperatures, as it is not only protected from evaporation, but also a network of subterranean canals (qanats) some 5,000 km long carries the waters from the nearby snow-covered Tien Shan into the fields, which are used mostly for viticulture.

GOBI   On some maps, the Gobi covers almost the whole of Central Asia's arid region, and the Takla Makan is only part of the Gobi. Other geographers consider them to be two separate deserts of equal importance. Théodore Monod, however, limits the Gobi to the steppe-like regions in the south of the Mongolian People's Republic and the north of the autonomous province of Inner Mongolia (which belongs to China). Its border here is the Ala Shan desert to the south. The confusion that is linked to the name 'Gobi' is certainly due at least in part to the fact that in the Chinese-Mongolian regions the word is not a name but describes a form of landscape. The rock and stone deserts that are typical of Central Asia are called *Gobis*, and the sand deserts are called *Shamos*.

The Gobi itself is more a kind of sandy steppe than a real desert. However, the many dune regions, which are very distinct from the rest and are called *Els* in Mongolia, create a strong desert-like impression in many parts of the Gobi, even though they account for only three per cent of the area. The monotony of the steppes is relieved by a large number of lakes, some of which are extremely salty. The winter temperature in the Gobi falls very low, frequently going down to minus 40ºC. A dry summer will always be followed by an extremely cold winter, which causes heavy losses among the herds of horses, sheep and camels. The Mongols call this *Zud*.

Scale: 1 cm = 150 km

BEI SHAN   The presence of certain flora and fauna and also the geological structure have led Théodore Monod to classify the Bei Shan as another Central Asian desert. He regards this mainly mountainous region as a link between the Sinkiang and the Gobi. Its western boundary lies east of Lop Nor; to the south it ends at the Nan Shan Mountains, to the north at the Mongolian border, and to the east at the Edsin Gol River. The arid, barren landscape is now crossed by a road that joins eastern China to the province of Sinkiang.

ALA SHAN   Adjoining the east of the Bei Shan desert is the Ala Shan, which extends as far as the Yellow River. In the north it reaches to the Mongolian border, and in the south to the line of the Nan Shan Mountains. Here too there is a certain amount of disagreement over terminology. Some experts speak of the Ala Shan Gobi, and say that the Ala Shan is part of the Gobi, although the latter term is meant to designate the form of the landscape. Others reject the term Ala Shan altogether, as Shan actually means mountains, and they divide this region between the Badain-Jaran and Tengger (Mongolian for 'wide sky') deserts. In its western part, a massive dune area has been formed, with megadunes that reach up to 430 m in height – among the tallest in the world. Among these dunes are over one hundred lakes whose salt content varies. Lake Yinderitu, which is surrounded by yellow dunes, is regarded as sacred by the Mongolian people.

ORDOS   The Ordos desert is technically a steppe, and is framed by a huge bend in the Yellow River. It covers an area of 300,000 km$^2$, and from west to east enjoys an increasing amount of rainfall, with the result that its economic exploitation changes from intensive cattle-farming to agriculture.

QAIDAM   The Qaidam desert is also virtually unknown. It lies north of the Plateau of Tibet, and maps and satellite photos show clearly that it is a basin. The Chinese call it the Qaidam Pendi (Chinese for basin), and it is 2,600–3,300 m above sea level, while the mountains around it rise to a height of 6,000 m. The Qaidam is full of mineral resources such as natural gas. A typical feature of the Qaidam is its salt lakes, the most important of which is Koko Nur, partly because of its size and partly because the Tibetans regard it as sacred.

TIBET   Tibet is a name to conjure up many associations, but 'desert' is not normally one of them. However, the western and central regions of Tibet show all the characteristics of desert country. Anyone travelling from Nepal to Tibet will see how effectively the Indian monsoon is kept out by the Himalayas.

A Tibetan youth carrying his sister across a pass.

The most pious Tibetan pilgrims go round the holy mountain of Kailash by measuring out the 52 km route

with their bodies. Their prostrations during this circuit are an important step along the path to enlightenment.

On the Nepalese side the slopes are covered with dense tropical forests, whereas to the north lies the desert-like Plateau of Tibet. The most arid region of Tibet is the Chang Tang desert, deep in the heart of the plateau, and in many places there are sand dunes, while there is not a single tree over an area of more than a million square kilometres.

THE SILK ROAD   A term that is most closely associated with the deserts of Central Asia, and which has for centuries sparked the imaginations of scholars and travellers alike is the Silk Road. The term was first coined in the nineteenth century by the German geographer Ferdinand von Richthofen (1833–1905), and it describes the route taken for a thousand years by traders travelling between China and the West. It was in fact a network of routes which the caravans used according to the nature of their goods, the safety of the journey, and the weather conditions. The oldest road went south, linking China with India and southeast Asia, whereas the oldest road to Europe went north starting out from Gansu north of the Tien Shan Mountains, through the forests of southern Asiatic Russia, and on to the mouth of the Don on the Black Sea.

The southern caravan route to which Ferdinand von Richthofen gave the name the Silk Road was actually the newest of these roads. In Dunhuang it split into two forks: the southern led across the Yangyuan Pass into the Tarim Basin, from there through Loulan and Kothan to Kashgar, and on to the Pamirs, where in a high valley it linked up with the northern branch. The latter left Chinese territory at the Jadetor Pass, across the Turpan Oasis, and reached the Pamirs via Kurla, Aksu and Kashgar.

Reunited, the Silk Road then went on through the Pamirs to Baktra – now Balkh, in Afghanistan – Merv, in present-day Turk-menistan, and Palmyra, in present-day Syria. From here, the various goods would be transported far and wide, to Alexandria, Attalaya (now Antalya), Petra and Rome. In Rome, Chinese silk was such a treasured commodity that in the year AD 16 the Senate had to forbid the wearing of silk garments in order to stem the loss of foreign currency. Even during the second and third centuries, the Romans still did not know how silk was made. For 2,000 years the Chinese managed to keep the process secret, and this was a major factor in the power of the Chinese Empire during the first few centuries AD. The Golden Age of the Silk Road was when the great Roman and Persian Empires and the Han and Tang Dynasties of China enjoyed such political stability that the safety of the traders and their caravans could be guaranteed.

Modern China extends far beyond the borders of the old Chinese Empire. Inner Mongolia in 1947, East Turkestan in 1949, and Tibet in 1950 were all occupied and annexed. Chinese occupation has had a major impact on the development of the Central Asian deserts, as well as the lives of the peoples that have lived in them since time immemorial – the Uyghuri, and the peoples of Kyrgyz, Uzbek, Kazakh, Tibet and Mongolia, to name but a few. The changes to infrastructure, such as the construction of motorways, airports and railways, have altered the face of the landscape considerably and have helped to facilitate the exploitation of raw materials.

In the Central Asian deserts that belong to China, there are now two parallel economic and social worlds. In one are the oasis farmers and cattle farmers, who still live and work mainly in the traditional manner; in the other are the predominantly Chinese inhabitants of rapidly expanding towns such as Korla, Hotan and Hohot, who have moved to the west of the country because of better career prospects and wages. The native people sometimes lead a shadowy existence in these towns: many of their old residential areas are being demolished to make way for prefabricated units. The yurts or tents of the herdsmen are often within sight of the great concrete blocks.

A very different development is to be observed in the Mongolian People's Republic. After the break-up of the Soviet Union, many Mongolians were forced to go back to the tradition of cattle farming. In fact, during the summer months about seventy per cent of the Mongolian population now live in yurts. Anyone travelling to the region could well get the feeling that he or she is back in the times of Genghis Khan. The horse is once again the main form of transport in the desert steppes of the Gobi, and in the Altai people still hunt with eagles.

In the Mongolian Altai, on the edge of the Gobi desert, Kazakhs use trained eagles to hunt for hares and foxes.

The Sunday market in Kashgar is the biggest in Central Asia.

At countless stalls Uyghuri sell kebabs and filled pastries.

The headlong rush towards modernization in China has left very few

traditional Uyghuri teahouses in Kashgar.

A Tibetan pilgrim goes round the holy lake of
Koko Nur, in the Qaidam desert, on his motorbike.

A young Mongolian herdsman rounds up his family's horses. Livestock farming by the nomads is still the most important industry in Mongolia.

The faces of the Ladakh nomads are often etched with the harshness of their living conditions.

In winter, temperatures fall to 40°C below zero, and the lack of oxygen is exhausting.

The poplar groves so typical of the oases in Central Asia are fed with water from the Indus, which rises in the

Kailash Mountains and flows through Ladakh. The colouring of the leaves heralds the harsh winter.

Many families send a son to one of the numerous monasteries in Ladakh,

which unlike those in Tibet have not been destroyed.                    117

The Shyok River flows through the Nubra
Valley. At the end of this valley rises the
Siachen Glacier.

Thousands of Tibetan pilgrims congregate on the holy mountain of Kailash

to celebrate the Festival of Saga-Dawa in honour of the Buddha.

During the days before the Festival of Saga-Dawa, many thousands of pilgrims from all over Tibet
go round the holy mountain of Kailash. The circuit stretches for 52 km and leads across passes
that are 5,000 m high. Most of the pilgrims accomplish this walk without a break.

The main ridge of the Himalayas keeps the rain clouds of the Indian monsoon away from Tibet,

so that large expanses of the Tibetan Plateau are deserts.

The harsh living conditions of the Tibetan
nomads are reflected in the expression of this
youth. He will have to endure the high altitude
and the freezing temperatures in winter.

A herd of yaks graze on a dune against the background of a Himalayan crest. Yaks are at the very centre of the Tibetan nomads' way of life.

# THE DESERTS OF AUSTRALIA

TANAMI DESERT

**GREAT SANDY DESERT**

GIBSON DESERT

**SIMPSON DESERT**

STURT STONY DESERT

TIRARI DESERT

STRZELECKI DESERT

**GREAT VICTORIA DESERT**

NULLARBOR PLAIN

# OVERVIEW OF AUSTRALIA

Australia is often described as the most arid of all the inhabited continents. Eighty per cent of its total area of 7.7 million square kilometres is arid or semi-arid, although this indicates little about the nature of the deserts themselves. In the whole of Australia there is not a single region that does not receive a yearly long-term average rainfall of at least 125 mm, whereas precipitation does not come even close to that figure in the Sahara. There are deserts and there are deserts, and indeed there are many different definitions that depend not only on objective factors such as climate, vegetation and geomorphology, but also on the personal criteria applied by the geographer. The yardstick used by most Australian experts is whether land is climatically suited to cultivation or not: all land that lies beyond the agronomic boundary is classified as desert. In the south, this means an annual rainfall of approximately 250 mm, and in the north 380 mm. A glance at the map will show a whole sequence of deserts whose names and boundaries often seem confusing or even contradictory. They were sometimes defined by nineteenth-century travellers and explorers who did not have the means to obtain a proper overview of the interior of the continent. Today, however, thanks to satellite pictures, one can distinguish two vast sand masses that are separated by a north-south corridor along which runs the Stuart Highway. West of this are the Great Sandy, the Gibson, the Tanami, the Great Victoria and the Nullarbor (i.e. treeless) Plain; east are the Simpson and its various adjacent regions. All these deserts are tropical.

# THE GREAT SANDY DESERT,
# THE GREAT VICTORIA DESERT
# AND THEIR SURROUNDINGS

Australia's situation on the tropic of Capricorn would lead one to expect tropical deserts like the Sahara in Africa. This, however, is countered by the fact that Australia is an island, and so there is a relatively moderate degree of aridity. The continent is generally flat, offering access on virtually all sides to moist air masses – particularly tropical masses coming from the north and north-west, which can bring heavy rainfall during the summer months. The arid south and southwest are affected by the west wind drift, which leads to maximum rainfall in the winter. An additional influence on the west coast is the lack of any substantial cold ocean current, such as those that create coastal deserts in America and Africa.

This chapter will look at those desert regions of Australia that lie west of the corridor where the Stuart Highway runs from Darwin to Port Augusta. These are the Great Sandy, the Gibson, the Tanami, the Great Victoria and the Nullarbor Plain.

THE GREAT SANDY DESERT is the largest in Australia and, together with the adjacent Gibson desert to the south, it covers an area of 600,000 km². Many geographers regard the Gibson desert as part of the Great Sandy. The area stretches from the Indian Ocean to the mountains of the McDonnell range; in the north, it reaches the foothills of the Kimberleys, and in the south the Warburton range.

The name itself describes the nature of this desert, which comprises a vast array of regular, parallel dunes that run from east to west and move 400–2,400 m a year. Their height varies between 15 and 30 m. Apart from a few scattered Aboriginal Australian communities and the Telfer goldmine, the Great Sandy is uninhabited and is crossed by rarely used tracks. The best known of these is the Canning Stock Route. This follows an old cattle route laid by Albert Canning in 1908–9. He bored fifty-two wells so that the cattle could be provided with enough

Sand and ashes after a bushfire.

Indian
Ocean

Darwin

Kimberleys

Broome

Halls Creek

TANAMI DESERT

GREAT SANDY DESERT

McDonnell Range

Alice Springs

GIBSON
DESERT

Ayers Rock

GREAT VICTORIA DESERT

NULLARBOR PLAIN

Perth

water, and they would be driven from Hall Creek to southwestern Australia on a journey that would take months. Losses were high, and it was not until 1930 that the route was used regularly. Even today, it takes a cross-country vehicle a good fortnight to travel the 1,750 km of the Canning Stock Route.

THE GIBSON DESERT was discovered by Ernest Giles (1835–97), who in 1873 named it after Alfred Gibson, who had died while attempting to cross it with Giles. It is famous for the wild flowers that grow there after the rainfall in spring. But even during the other seasons, it is difficult to regard the Gibson or the Great Sandy as real deserts, as grass and other vegetation proliferate. The most common is spinifex, which grows in densely clustered circular mounds. It is hard and sharp-edged, which makes it extremely difficult to get at. The most common tree is the mulga, a thornless acacia. Around fifty per cent of Australian plant life is endemic, having evolved in isolation.

THE TANAMI DESERT lies northeast of the Great Sandy, and owes its name to the Tanami goldmine. In contrast to the Great Sandy, it consists mainly of gravel, but it too is regarded by many geographers as just a part of the Great Sandy.

South of the Great Sandy, Tanami and Gibson deserts is the Great Victoria. This covers an area of 350,000 km², and

stretches out 1,300 km from the Stuart Highway to the west. It is a dry, flat region covered in rows of dunes, which are shorter and less regular than those in the Great Sandy. The average annual rainfall is more than 200 mm, and consequently the dunes tend to be more or less covered with vegetation.

THE GREAT VICTORIA DESERT is crossed by the so-called Bomb Roads, which were built in the 1950s as part of the infrastructure for rocket tests in Woomera and nuclear tests in Emu. Len Beadell (1923–95) has become legendary in Australia, as he was the pioneer who built the single-lane roads across the Great Victoria, naming them the Ann Beadell Highway and the Connie Sue Highway after his wife and daughter.

NULLARBOR PLAIN   In the south, the Nullarbor Plain borders on the Great Victoria. This is a treeless, limestone plain that ends abruptly in a sheer drop to the ocean. It stretches 920 km from east to west, and 320 km from north to south, and is crossed by the Indian Pacific railway, which runs in an absolutely straight line for 480 km.

There are marked differences between the two great Australian desert regions as far as the inhabitants and their settlements are concerned. East of the corridor through which the Stuart Highway runs, white Australians live in farms known

Scale: 1 cm = 100 km

as 'stations' or in small communities, whereas the western desert regions are inhabited almost exclusively by Aboriginal Australians. Their communities are all very similar in structure and architecture because their settlements, rather than being natural, were purpose-built by the State. In addition to private homes, there are administration buildings, schools, and social and medical centres.

With limited work and prospects, many Aboriginal Australians are driven into the cities. These communities are often marked by additional problems, such as alcoholism, particularly among young Aboriginal Australians. Life expectancy and general state of health tend to be on a par with the poorest African states.

The communities have been built on Aboriginal freehold land, which was given back to them after a long struggle. However, many leaders now regard it as a major mistake to have concentrated on the political fight for the restoration of the land without having also fought for the chance of a proper economic future.

The Gary Highway is part of the Bomb Roads, which were used for atomic-weapon and rocket tests in the 1950s.

Ayers Rock (Uluru) is in the centre of Australia and is the largest monolith on Earth.

The Aboriginal Australians regard it as sacred.

Trees throw their shadows over the sandstone of Ayers Rock, which is reddened by ferric oxide. The rock is still called officially by its Aboriginal Australian name of Uluru.

Aboriginal Australian communities are often located in quite remote places.

In the deserts of Australia, bushfires are a part of the ecosystem.

Their main victim is the dry grass, and most trees manage to survive.

# THE SIMPSON DESERT
# AND ITS SURROUNDINGS

The heart of the Simpson desert covers an area of 50,000 km$^2$. Théodore Monod regards the neighbouring regions in the south-east – known as the Sturt Stony desert, the Tirari desert and the Strzelecki desert – as part of the Simpson, which would give it a total area of 300,000 km$^2$.

Apart from the gravel of the Sturt Stony, all of them consist predominantly of sand dunes, which makes the Simpson the world's best-known example of a sand-ridge desert. There are more than a thousand of these ridges, many of which stretch for hundreds of kilometres. The dunes are not active. For the most part, they were formed during the arid phases of the Pleistocene Epoch, the last of which was between 12,000 and 18,000 BC. Since then, they have become stabilized by vegetation. The only active dunes are now found in the central areas of the Simpson and the Strzelecki. Dunes are formed by either water or wind piling the sand into a heap. The ridges in the Simpson desert –

where rivers carried great quantities of sediment from the high-lands into lakes that had no outlet – are more even and sandy than in the western regions, where the sand derived mainly from the erosion of existing stone. The sandy material that had been deposited in the lakes gradually spread along the shores, piled up, and was eventually blown away.

The eastern and southern regions are still permeated with salt lakes, the largest of which is Lake Eyre. The Warburton River reaches this lake every two or three years, but there has only been enough water to fill the gigantic basin (which covers 8,430 km$^2$) three times in the last 150 years – in 1950, 1974 and 2000. When this happens, the layer of salt in Lake Eyre, up to 46 m thick, is completely dissolved – a major event when you consider that it involves no less than 400 million tonnes of salt.

The lakes and river systems in the south and east of the Simpson desert are bound up with the existence of a colossal

The airfield at Birdsville on the day of the famous horse race.

SIMPSON
DESERT

McDonnell Range
• Alice Springs

• Birdsville

STURT STONY
DESERT

Oodnadatta •

TIRARI
DESERT

STRZELECKI
DESERT

Lake
Eyre

William
Creek •

• Marree

• Cooper Pedy

Flinders Range

reservoir of groundwater: the Great Artesian Basin. This covers an area of 1.8 million square kilometres, and is the biggest groundwater reservoir in the world. In some places, the water emerges from Artesian springs, and in others wells have been sunk to pump Artesian water out with wind turbines. A particularly impressive example is Mound Springs, where the water emerges from the tops of about one hundred little hills. In the water are various minerals – including carbonate, sulphate and chloride – and these gradually form a deposit that builds up the mounds. This continues until the Artesian pressure is no longer strong enough to bring the water up.

These Artesian wells, which can go down to a depth of 2,000 m, were essential for the establishment of the cattle farms on the edge of the Simpson desert. One of these, the Anna Creek Station, is the biggest farm on Earth, covering 34,000 km² – approximately the size of Belgium. A manager and thirteen stockmen look after 13,000 head of cattle, which are herded from pasture to pasture with the aid of all-terrain motorbikes and mini-helicopters. Vegetation is sparse, and allows for only one cow per square kilometre.

West of Anna Creek Station, on the Stuart Highway, is Cooper Pedy – one of the centres of Australian opal mining, where prospectors from all over the world stake their claims for a small fee and go in search of riches. Some sites are explored with mobile drills, and others with bulldozers.

The majority of the settlements on the edge of the Simpson and in the surrounding regions consist of just a few houses. The building of a railway running west has robbed such places as Marree, Oodnadatta and Williams Creek of their importance. However, the remains of the legendary Ghan railway – the name derives from the Afghans who opened up the outback in the nineteenth century with their camels – attract many thousands of tourists every year. They follow the old cattle routes of Oodnadatta, Birdsville and Strzelecki in cross-country vehicles.

Birdsville, on the eastern periphery of the Simpson desert, is right in the middle of the outback, far from any tarmac road and populated by a mere 200 people. Yet, during the first weekend in September it is the scene of a famous horse race which brings vast crowds from all over the continent. At this time, Birdsville's airfield is the most popular airport in Australia.

Scale: 1 cm = 75 km

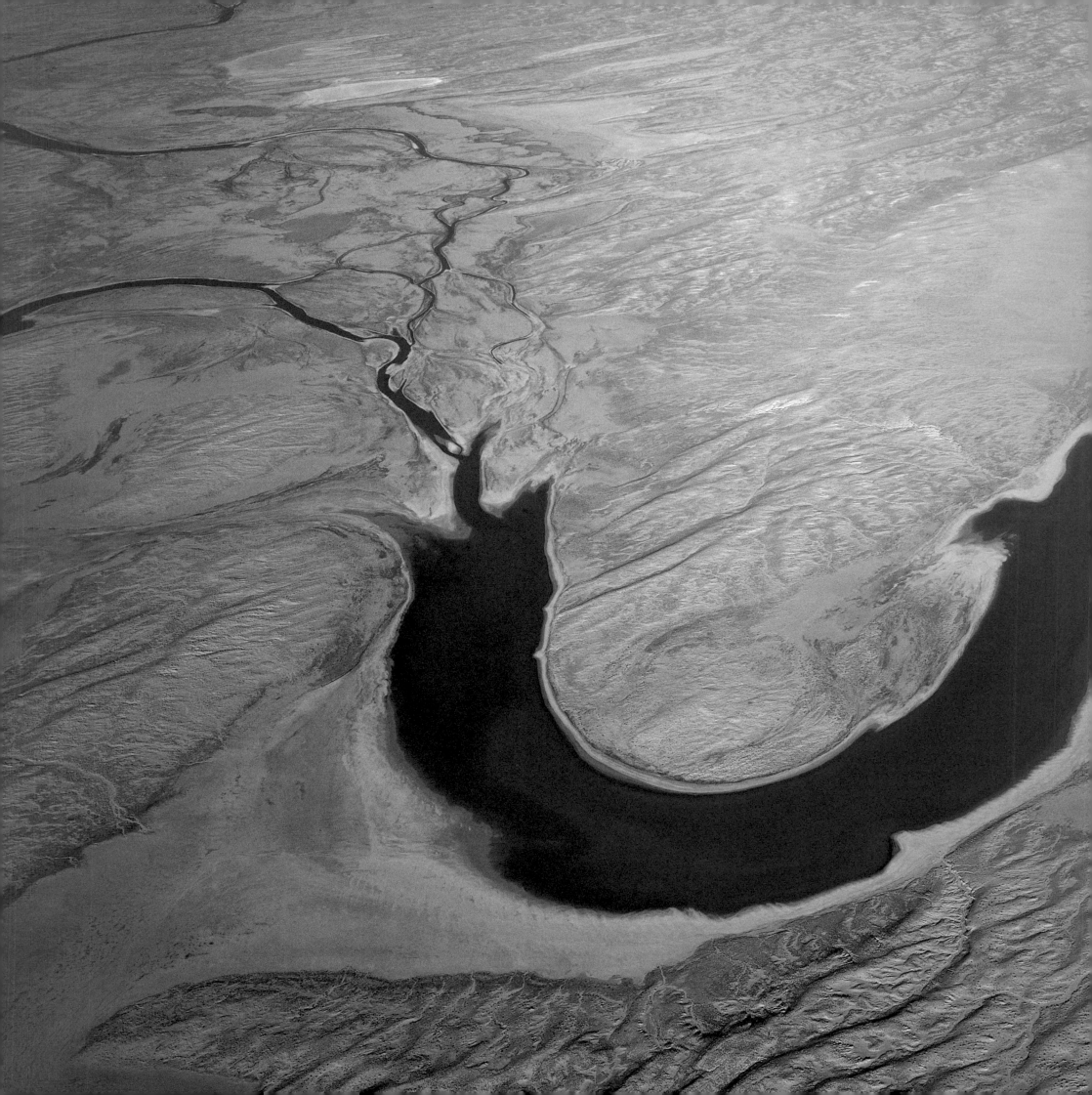

Only rarely does the Warburton River reach
Lake Eyre. Three times in the last century so
much water flowed into the lake that the 400
million tonnes of salt in the lake dissolved.

From the air it looks as if the drill holes of the opal miners at Cooper Pedy are haphazard.

However, they are all based on the hope of finding rich veins of opal in particular areas.

Twice a year, thousands of cattle are rounded up at

Anna Creek – the largest cattle farm in the world –

in order to count, select and brand the animals.

The salt layer in Lake Eyre is up to 46 m thick. In some places it is broken by springs that are rich in minerals. Aerial photo from 100 m up.

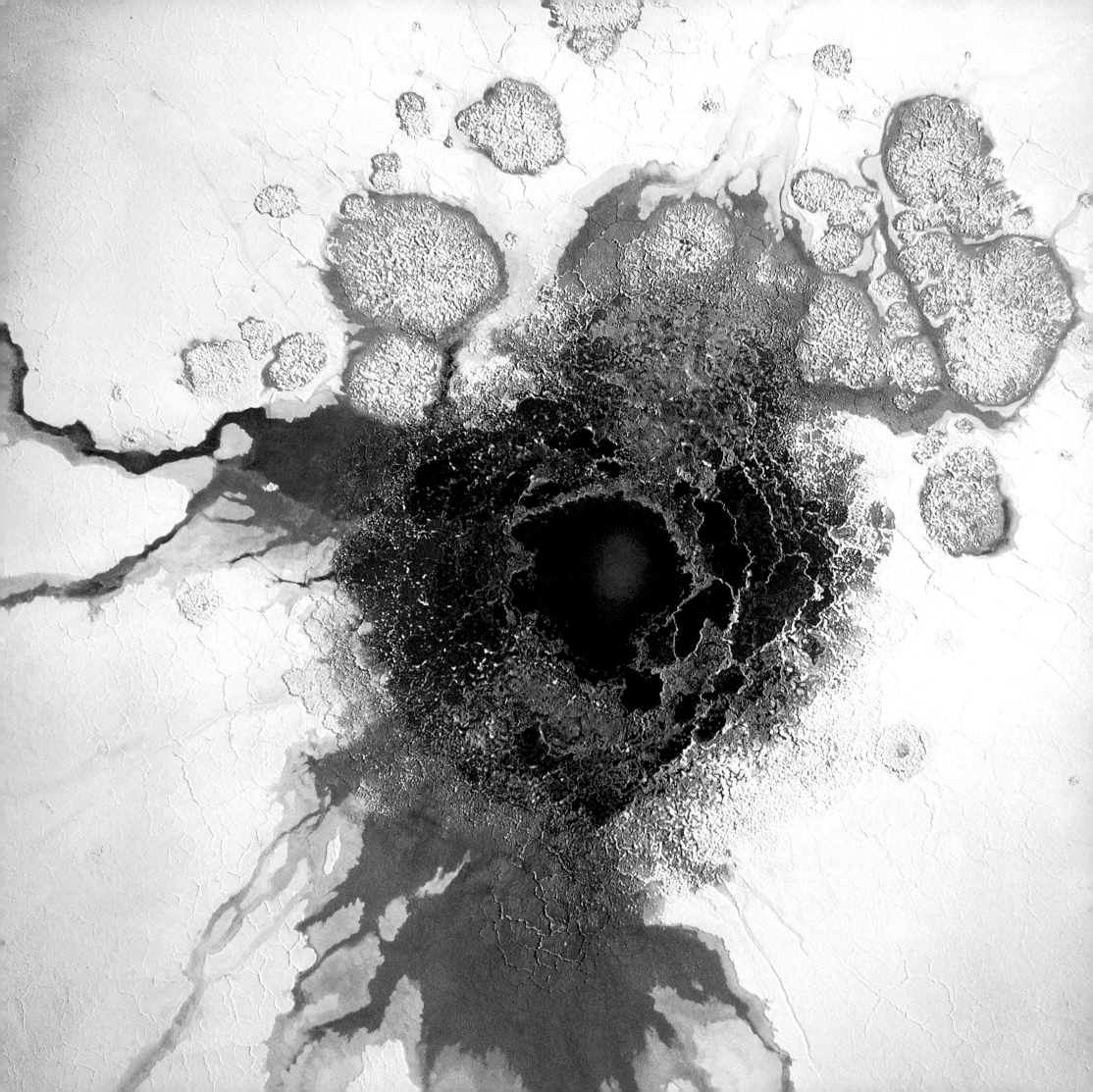

# THE DESERTS OF AMERICA

GREAT
BASIN
DESERT

MOJAVE

SONORA

CHIHUAHUA
DESERT

PERUVIAN COASTAL DESERT

ATACAMA

PATAGONIAN DESERT

# OVERVIEW OF AMERICA

Only 19.5 per cent of the total area of North and South America is desert or semi-desert – the smallest proportion of all the continents. The arid zones occupy 7.6 million square kilometres, of which almost 4.3 million are in the North and 3.4 million in the South. The actual proportions are 20 per cent in the North and 19 per cent in the South. As far as the hyper-arid regions are concerned, the area covers a mere two per cent. The vast meridional expanse of the Americas – which are traversed by the tropics of both Cancer and Capricorn – brings with it a corresponding variety of climates. The aridity of the North American deserts is determined by the relief. In South America, the Andes have a decisive influence on the nature of the deserts along the South American Arid Diagonal. The effects that cold currents, such as the Humboldt and the California, have on the climate should definitely not be underestimated, however.

The North American deserts are in northern Mexico and the southwest of the USA. The Mojave and the Great Basin are in the USA, while the Sonora and the Chihuahua straddle both regions. The deserts of South America stretch along the Arid Diagonal, which runs from northern Peru 5,000 km to the Patagonian Atlantic coast. The Atacama, a typical coastal desert, is part of this belt. Two isolated South American arid zones are relatively rich in vegetation and so can scarcely be called deserts: the wind-swept northern coast of Venezuela with its offshore islands, and the Sertao in northeastern Brazil. In both cases, the climatic causes of aridity are extremely complex.

Scale: 1 cm = 400 km

# THE DESERTS OF NORTH AMERICA

There are four major deserts in North America: the Chihuahua, the Mojave, the Sonora and the Great Basin. As they are all very accessible, they are among the best-researched deserts in the world, and consequently there is an abundance of literature and maps. However, you will scarcely find two books, essays or maps that agree on the borders of the individual deserts. The names themselves are used not only to denote geological and tectonic entities, but also to cover the different regions according to their vegetation. In addition, American geographers have a much broader concept of what constitutes 'desert' than their European colleagues, who can boast the Sahara – a 'real' desert, in the proper sense of the word – at the very gateway to Europe. The Americans also distinguish between high and low desert, a distinction that is particular to America.

The aridity of the North American deserts is influenced mainly by factors of structural relief. The two main sections of the Cordilleras, for instance, in the southwest of the USA, are separated by a massive gap: between the Pacific mountain ranges in the west and the Rocky Mountains in the east stretches a vast intermontane zone of plateaux and basins. The Pacific mountain ranges effectively keep out the moist air from the ocean, so that rainfall on the leeward side is of desert proportions. The same effect is to be seen in the Mexican highlands, where the Sierra Madre Occidental is blocked off from the moist air of the Pacific. Here the aridity is further increased by proximity to the tropic of Cancer.

In both the intermontane zone of the USA and the Mexican highlands, the relief is characterized by the sequence of basins and ranges. There are extended ranges with basins in between, and the latter get very little rainfall owing to their position on the leeward side of the mountains. This applies to the majority of North American deserts.

GREAT
BASIN
DESERT

Salt Lake City

Great
Salt Lake

USA

San Francisco

Sierra Nevada

Canyon-
lands

Colorado

Death Valley

Las Vegas

Monument
Valley

Ship Rock

MOJAVE
DESERT

Plateau

Los Angeles

Quartzsite

Phoenix

White
Sands

Pinacate

SONORA
DESERT

El Paso

CHIHUAHUA

Baja California

Gulf of California

Sierra Occidental

DESERT

Sierra Oriental

Rio Grande

Pacific

MEXICO

It should also be mentioned that the aridity of the Lower Californian peninsula is caused not only by its situation on the tropic of Cancer, but also by the cold California current.

CHIHUAHUA   The Chihuahua, named after the state in Mexico, is the southernmost desert in North America. South of the Rio Grande, it incorporates the Mexican highlands that rise sharply to the south, and is enclosed by the mountain ranges of the Sierra Madre Oriental and Occidental. About a third of the Chihuahua extends north across the great bend of the Rio Grande, spreads southwest of Texas, and juts out in two sections into southern New Mexico. The Mexican part of the Chihuahua is more arid, because sinking air movements over the tropic of Cancer combine with the relief to reduce rainfall drastically. As already mentioned, the Sierra Madre Occidental on the western side of the desert keeps out the winter storms that arise in the Gulf of California. It is a similar story in the east, where the lofty Sierra Madre Oriental blocks the path of the winds from the Gulf of Mexico, and the storms are only able to cross these heights and bring some rain to the region during the summer months.

There are several forms of vegetation in the Chihuahua: waves of grassland in the volcanic soil, creosote bushes on the plains, cactus savannas, and agaves in the limestone areas. The most unusual landscape of all is the Tularosa Basin in New Mexico. The dunes of White Sands stretch over an area of 770 km$^2$. They are snow white, and the sand is made of gypsum and not quartz. Although gypsum can be found in all deserts, nowhere else on Earth has such an expanse of gypsum dunes. Their formation is closely linked to the recent geological history of the Tularosa Basin. Once the depression had been formed, the rivers came pouring down from the surrounding mountains to create a huge lake. Their waters carried minerals with them – above all gypsum. After the end of the last Ice Age, the lake began to dry out because of rising temperatures. Evaporation isolated the gypsum, which formed itself into crystals, and even today the winds continue to pile these up into dunes. More than sixty species of plant have managed to adapt themselves to life in the gypsum dunes.

SONORA   To the west of Chihuahua lies the Sonora. It covers 320,000 km$^2$, and reaches from southeast California and southwest Arizona to a latitude of 24° north. It encompasses both sides of the Gulf of California, covering the western half of the Mexican province of Sonora and almost the entire peninsula of Lower California. The height of the Sonora varies considerably: from the Lower Californian coast in the west it rises continuously to its eastern side, reaching 3,000 m above sea level. The temperatures are equally varied, though the Sonora ranks as one of the warm deserts. Rains come in winter from the storms over the Pacific, and in summer from the Gulf of Mexico, and the annual average is between 150 and 300 mm. The fact that there are two rainy seasons has given rise to the rich plant life of the Sonora. It boasts the largest number and the greatest variety of cacti in the world, with no less than twenty-seven types. The tallest are the candelabra (saguaro), which towers up in columns, and the organ-pipe.

The north of the Sonora is known as the Colorado Desert. The aridity of this region derives from its situation in a subtropical belt of high pressure, and this is reinforced by the current from the north, which affects the western side of the peninsula. Although it is one of the most arid areas of the Sonora, it has been possible to irrigate much of this desert thanks to the vast quantity of water carried by the Colorado River on its way to the Gulf of California. The Gulf of California divides the 1,300 km long peninsula of Lower California, which extends southwards from the Mexican mainland through the tropic of Cancer.

MOJAVE   Adjacent to the north of the Sonora is the Mojave desert. This is the smallest of the North American deserts, but also the most variable in height. Most of it lies in southeastern California, but it extends into southern Nevada and western Arizona. The Mojave itself is mountain country, with the Sierra Nevada to the west, and the San Bernardino Mountains – marking the separation from the Sonora – to the south. In the north and northeast are smaller ranges that form the border to the Great Basin Desert.

The Sierra Nevada and the San Bernardino Mountains seal the Mojave off from the moist Pacific winds, and very few winter storms manage to surmount these barriers. As a result, the Mojave has the lowest rainfall of all the North American deserts. In Barstow the average yearly rainfall is 100 mm, while in Death Valley it is barely 40 mm. It was in Death Valley, in July 1913, that the highest ever temperature was recorded: 57°C in the shade.

In geological terms, Death Valley – 200 km long and 10–59 km wide – is a rift valley (where the land has sunk between two more or less parallel faults in the Earth's crust). These disturbances in the Earth's surface are still active today, and they explain the enormous differences in height: Death Valley,

Antelope Canyon.

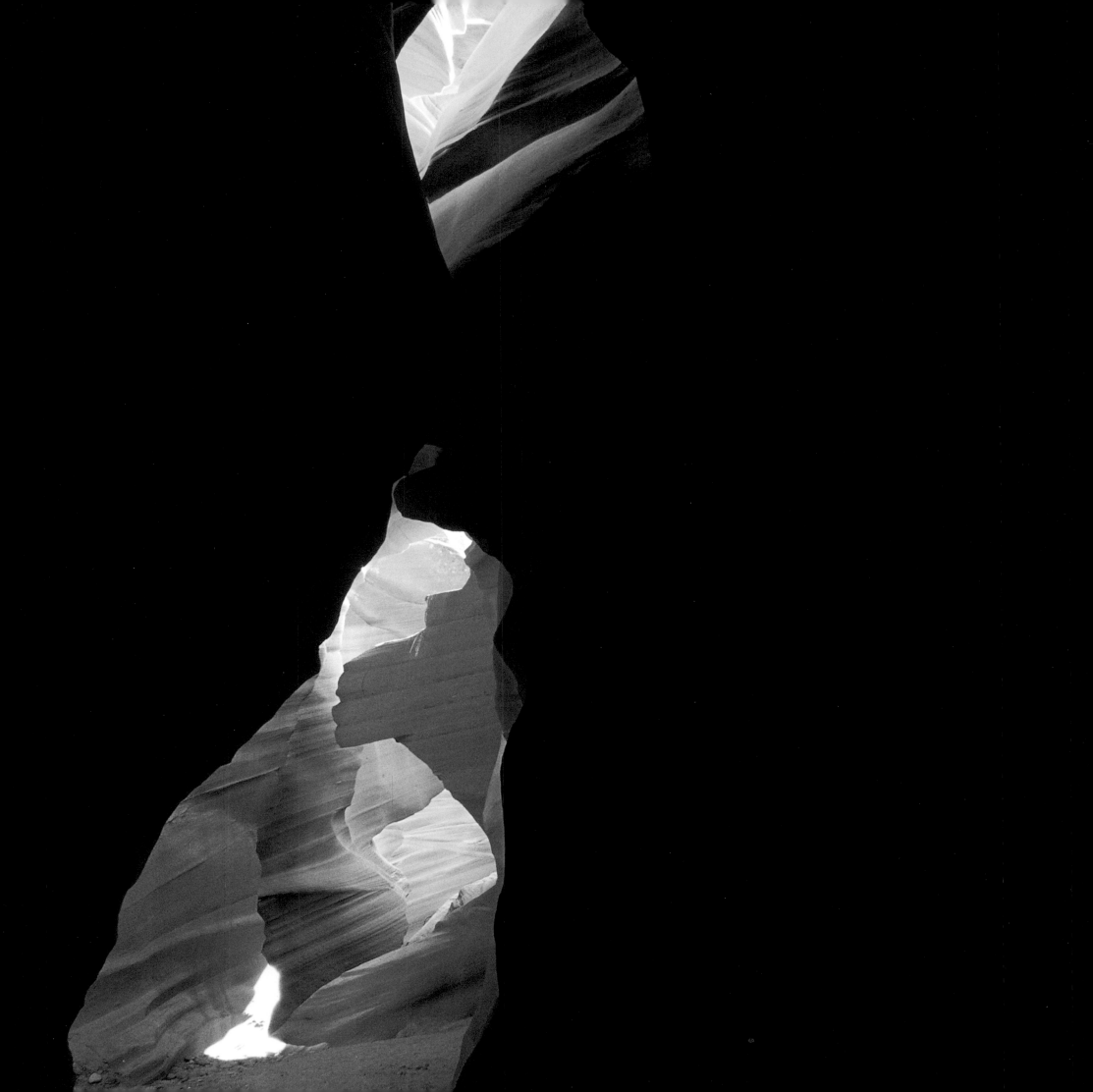

at 86 m below sea level, is the lowest point in America, and yet it opens out onto the 4,348 m high Mount Whitney. The landscapes here are also extremely varied: salt lakes, colourful canyons, sand dunes and playas can all be seen in close proximity to one another. One of the playas harbours a unique natural phenomenon: at the end of tracks that are 2.5 m deep and often run for hundreds of metres, there are rocks of different sizes, the largest of which weighs 45 kg. The shape of these rocks and the form of the tracks leave no doubt that the latter were scratched in the clay by the former. The cause of this migration – stones moving from the edge of the playa into the centre – has been the subject of much scholarly debate. One theory is that after heavy rainfall – when the surface of the playa becomes slippery – a strong wind must have blown the stones away. But no one has ever seen such an occurrence. Other, generally very complicated explanations involve the effects of ice.

Most of the Mojave lies at a height of between 600 and 1,200 m. In the lower areas, the landscape is dominated by creosote bushes, whereas higher up the most striking plant is the Joshua tree. This is a form of yucca unique to the Mojave, and it has a trunk which often branches out just above the base. At the end of each branch are short, jagged leaves that come together in a kind of bush. Joshua trees can grow up to 12 m tall, and are mostly found in large clusters.

GREAT BASIN DESERT   The Great Basin Desert lies to the north of the Mojave. The name is slightly misleading, as this is not a single depression but a series of basins in an intermontane zone clearly marked off by mountains to the east and west. There are numerous ranges running from north to south and reaching up to heights of 3,000 m, between which lie scores of independent drainage basins.

The Great Basin is the biggest single desert in North America, and extends to northeastern California, across most of Nevada and Utah, and parts of southeastern Oregon. The basins are between 1,000 and 1,500 m high, and the vegetation is dominated by wormwood and sagebrush, the latter of which gives way to saltbushes in the drier areas. The largest of the basins lies in the east, where Great Salt Lake is situated, with a vast expanse of desert all around it. This lake is a relic of one that was even bigger during the Ice Age – Lake Bonneville.

Although they are geologically very different from the Basin Range Province of the Great Basin, parts of the Colorado

Meteorite crater near Flagstaff.

Plateau are often grouped with the latter. The Colorado Plateau lies east of the Great Basin. It is about 200 m high, and has very little in common with other desert regions of North America. The plateau itself covers an area of 330,000 km², and is divided up into individual plateaux separated by steep banks and terraces. These are the most spectacular landscapes in the USA, attracting millions of tourists every year.

Living conditions in the deserts of North America are extremely variable. The main reason for this is the economic difference between Mexico and the USA – one which each year causes hundreds of thousands of Mexicans to try and cross the border that runs through the Sonora and Chihuahua deserts. There are also marked social differences between the American states themselves. The Arizona sun belt, with 300 days of sunshine in the year, attracts the rich and powerful from all parts of the USA. The millions of mobile homes that stand on permanent campsites or in the desert itself provide a stark contrast.

Most of the people who live in these deserts resist accepting such surroundings as their home. They do all they can to minimize the discomforts – such as the appalling heat in summer – with the aid of sophisticated technology. This is particularly true in large cities such as Las Vegas and Phoenix, which are dependent on a large number of dams for their enormous consumption of water and electricity. Phoenix gets its water from Lake Mead, a reservoir on the Colorado River, and its electricity from the Hoover Dam Power Station, which also supplies Los Angeles and Las Vegas.

Conditions could not be more different in the Native American reservations, most of which are situated on the Colorado Plateau and were set up at the beginning of the nineteenth century. The biggest of these is the Navajo reservation, which also encompasses the Hopi reservation and extends across Arizona to New Mexico, Utah and Colorado. Demographic pressures there have led to over-exploitation of poor-quality countryside.

Creosote bush in Death Valley.

On the slopes of the volcano Pinacate, in the Mexican Sonora desert,

the only plants to flourish in the low rainfall are organ-pipe cacti and certain bushes.

Every year, hundreds of thousands of pensioners leave the cold states of the USA

to spend the winter in the Sonora desert, living in their mobile homes.

The saguaro cactus has become an emblem of the Sonora desert.

It can live for several hundred years, grows up to 16 m in height,

and weighs more than 10 tonnes.

The Colorado River has cut deep into the stone strata of the Colorado Plateau, which extends over an area of 330,000 km². The river rises in the Rocky Mountains, flows southwest of the Colorado Plateau through the Sonora desert, and out into the Gulf of California in Mexico.

Over the course of millions of years,
weathering has caused huge blocks of stone
to break off from the massif overlooking
Lake Powell.

Monument Valley with its mesas, buttes and spires has come to symbolize

the arid southwest of the USA. North of here, on the San Juan River,

the folded layers of the Colorado Plateau are clearly visible from the air.

184

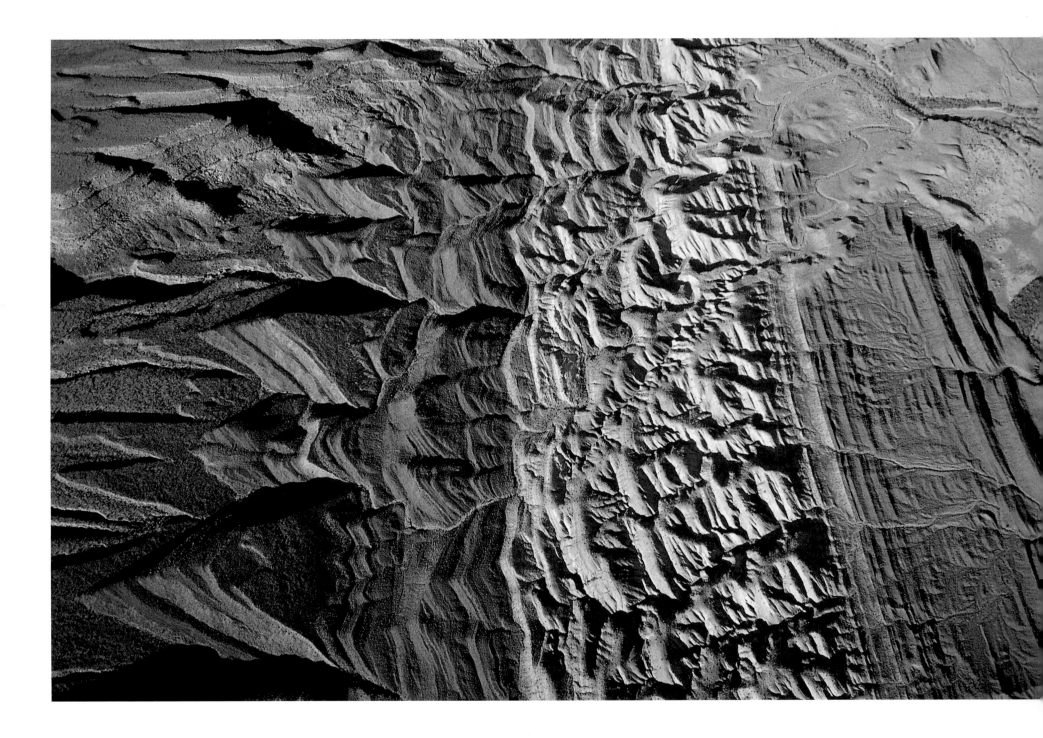

Sunrise on the mesa Arch, one of 2,000 such mesas in the Canyonlands.

Ship Rock, an extinct volcano in Four Corners, is the sacred mountain

of the Navajo Native Americans, who live to the west in the Navajo reservation.

On the Colorado Plateau, weathering and erosion have created

a wonderfully rich variety of forms. Aerial photo from 400 m.

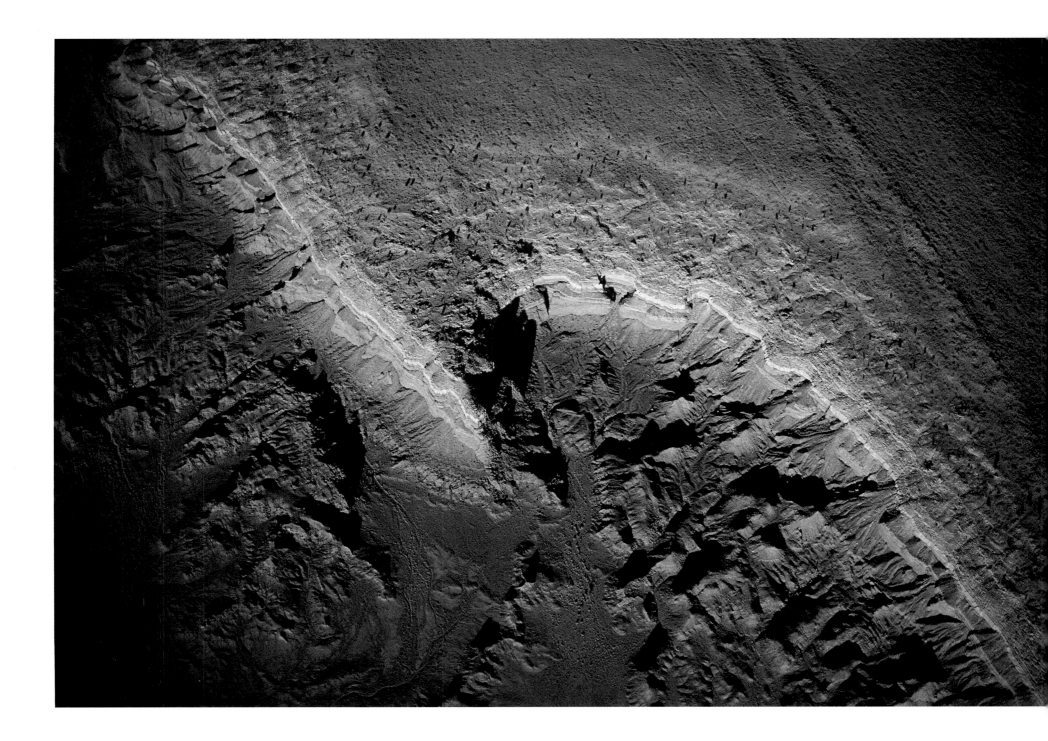

The erosive forces of wind and water have
sculpted the red sandstone of the Paria
Plateau into a spectacular wave.

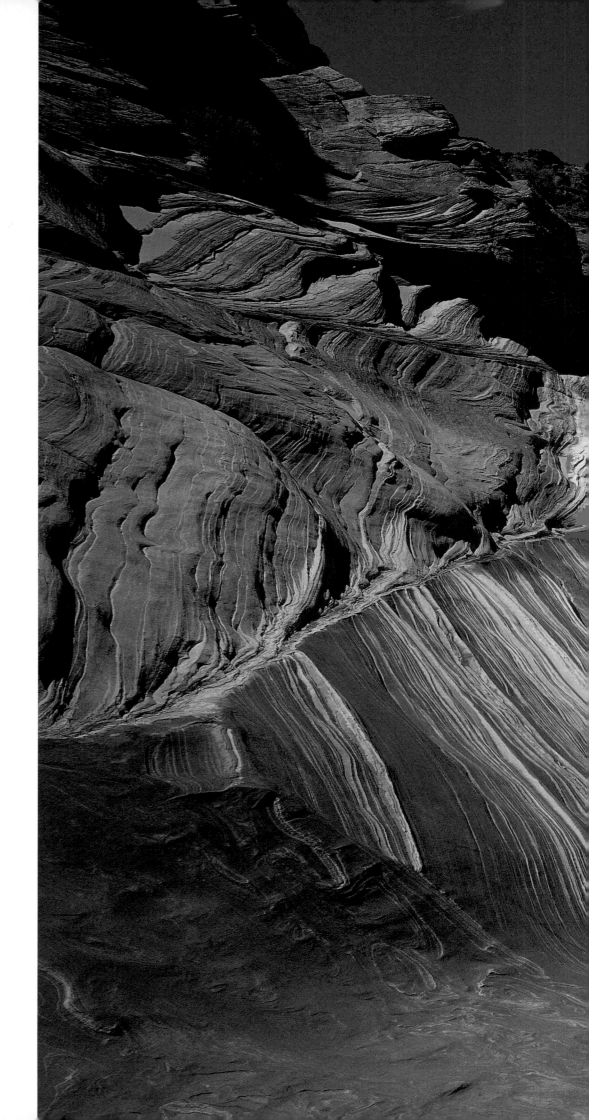

In a playa in Death Valley, there are tracks that are 2.5 cm deep and often run for hundreds of metres, at the end of which are large chunks of rock. No one has yet discovered how they get there, although new tracks are constantly being formed.

Among the unique gypsum dunes of White Sands there are over sixty varieties of plants,

including the soapberry yucca. This stretches its stem so that its leaves can rise above

the gypsum of the ever-growing dunes.

# THE DESERTS OF THE
# SOUTH AMERICAN ARID DIAGONAL

The South American Arid Diagonal runs from northwest to southeast, from northern Peru to the Atlantic coast of Patagonia, and it covers more than 5,000 km. In addition to the Atacama, it encompasses parts of the Bolivian Altiplano, and at a latitude of 24–26° south crosses the Andes before making its way east towards Patagonia.

Although this arid line represents a continual band of desert, its origins go back to different climatic events, and it boasts a huge variety landscapes. On the one hand, there is the narrow strip of the Atacama, which begins just 400 km south of the Equator and reaches as far as 25° south; on the other, there is an arid region that stretches diagonally from the Bolivian Altiplano across the Andes to Patagonia, thus extending far beyond the southern tip of the Atacama.

## THE ATACAMA AS PART OF THE SOUTH AMERICAN ARID

DIAGONAL  Many geographers limit the Atacama to its Chilean section, and regard the Peruvian Coastal Desert as an entity in itself. For others, however, the latter counts as part of the Atacama, because climatic conditions are so similar.

The aridity of the Atacama is due mainly to the cold Humboldt current that comes from the Antarctic. Other causes are the fact that this desert crosses the tropic of Capricorn, and is shielded by the Andes against the moist air masses from the Atlantic and the Amazon. The fact that the desert in northern Peru reaches to within a few hundred kilometres of the Equator, where one would expect permanent moisture, is due to the northwesterly bend in the Peruvian coastline, which results in the dry wind blowing parallel to the coast.

The entire length of the Atacama consists of a coastal zone and an inland zone, and from May to November the former is covered in a fog, which the Peruvians call *Garua* and the Chileans *Chamanchaca*. As the lower levels of air are colder

The El Tatio geyser on the Chilean Altiplano.

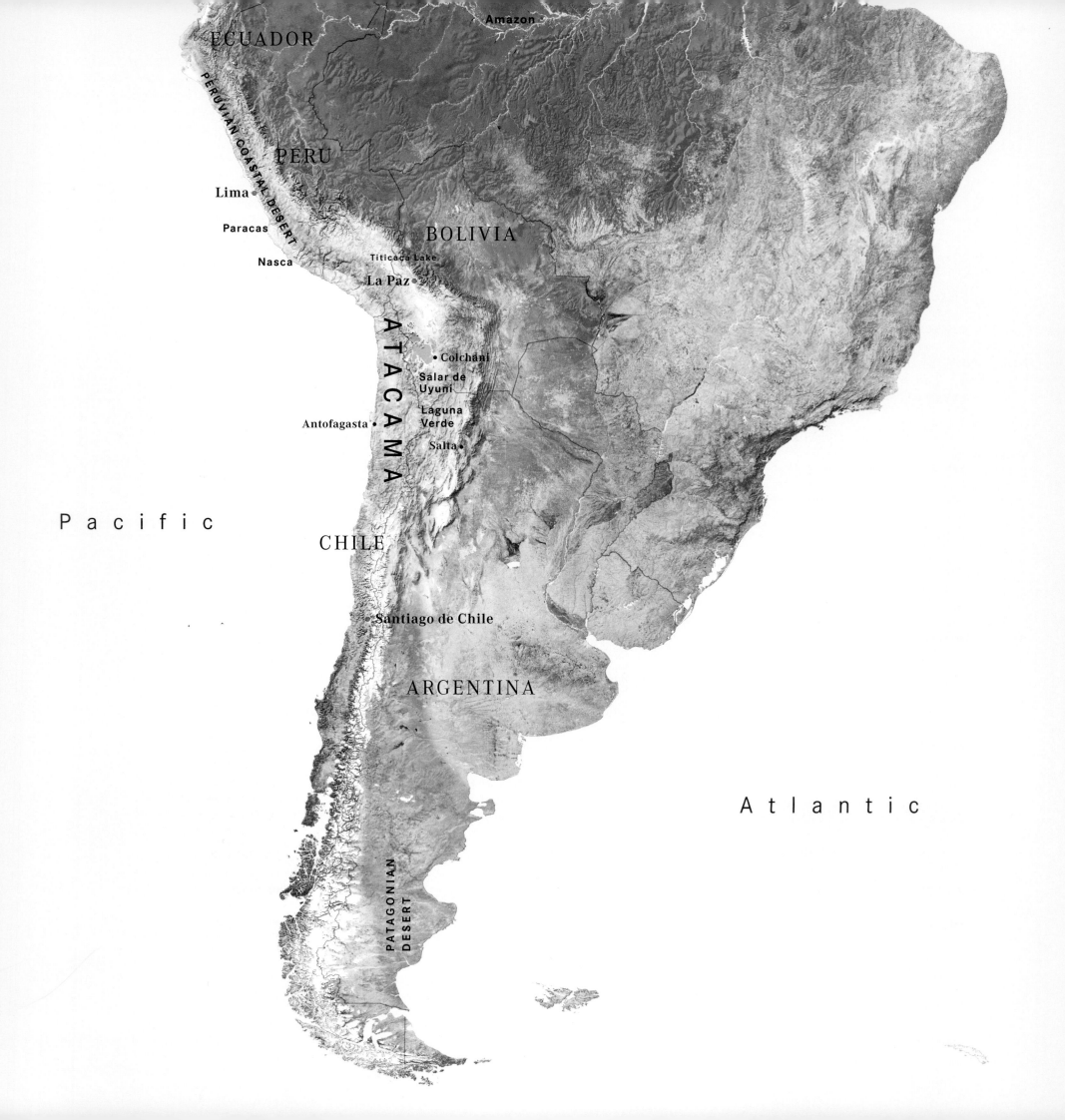

ECUADOR

PERU

PERUVIAN COASTAL DESERT

Lima

Paracas

Nasca

Amazon

BOLIVIA

Titicaca Lake

La Paz•

•Colchani

Salar de
Uyuni

Antofagasta•

Laguna
Verde

Salta•

A
T
A
C
A
M
A

Pacific

CHILE

Santiago de Chile•

ARGENTINA

PATAGONIAN
DESERT

Atlantic

than the upper (inversion), there is no rain despite the high degree of moisture in the air. Many places along the coast have seen no rain for years, and over the course of time the average often lies between one and five millimetres. The damp fog has caused the development of a very particular form of vegetation which is called *loma*, and most of these plants are endemic.

The coastal landscape is frequently shaped by Cordilleras, and in many places there are mighty dunes overlooking the sea. The fog reaches up to a height of 700–1,000 m above sea level, and that is the point at which the mainly sunny inland zone begins. This is one of the most arid regions in the world, for it lies beyond the foggy zone, and to the east the Andes form a barrier to keep out the moist air masses from the Atlantic. There is often no vegetation at all, as can be seen most strikingly in the impressive Chilean pampas of Tamarugal. Because of the very low moisture content of the air and the lack of clouds, the south of the Chilean inland desert was chosen to be the site of the European Observatory, along with other observatories focusing on the southern skies.

The only oases to be found in the Chilean Atacama are in the western foothills of the Cordilleras, and the exceptionally arid inland desert separates the Chilean coastal towns from these

oases. Water for Antofagasta therefore has to be piped 300 km from the Cordilleras. The situation is very different in Peru, where coastal towns are situated on river oases. These have grown up along the rivers that flow from the Andes, and the export-orientated cultivation of fruit constitutes a substantial part of the Peruvian economy.

Until the 1870s, guano was the most important export from the Atacama. This excrement from seabirds was highly prized in Europe as a fertilizer because of the high content of nitrogen – this was at a time when there were no artificial fertilizers. The availability of the guano was due to the absence of rain, which would otherwise have washed all the deposits away. When these were exhausted, however, nothing remained except what the birds provided day by day, and so production dwindled from 500,000 tonnes to the current level of less than 10,000.

After the Atacama guano boom came the saltpetre boom. This nitrate is to be found in the driest regions of the Chilean inland desert. There are no other viable saltpetre fields in the world, because the accumulation and preservation of these easily dissolved nitrates is only possible in the long-term aridity of this particular region. Saltpetre is used in the manufacture of fertilizer and gunpowder. At the beginning of the twentieth

Scale: 1 cm = 200 km.

The Paracas peninsula is part of the Peruvian Coastal Desert,
which owes its existence to the cold Humboldt current.
The hostile conditions of the coastal desert are in striking
contrast to the wealth of ocean fauna. The waters here are among
the richest fishing grounds in the world.

205

America
CHILE

The railway has opened up the mining regions of the Atacama.

Steam from the hot springs of Sol de Manana
rises into the ice-cold air of the Altiplano.
The sulphurous springs are the result of
continuous tectonic activity in the Andes.

209

The Laguna Verde changes its colour around midday
from whitish to glowing green. This phenomenon is
caused by the photochemical reactions of the algae
that live in the lake, which is in the shadow of the
volcano Licancabur.

The village of Colchani lies on the edge of the Salar de Uyuni. The salt that is
extracted here is pressed together by hand and sent away by rail.

On a cold winter's evening, the full moon rises over the salty plain of the Salar de Uyuni, the surface turning purple in the dusk. After the summer rains, the salt forms new, regular-shaped polygonal patterns.

SAHARA   DANAKIL-SOMALIA   CHALBI DESERT   KAISUT DESERT   KALAHARI   KAROO   NAMIB

# THE DESERTS OF AFRICA

SAHARA

DANAKIL

CHALBI
DESERT

KAISUT
DESERT

NAMIB

KALAHARI

KAROO

# OVERVIEW OF AFRICA

Of all the continents, Africa is certainly the one we would most associate with deserts. Fifty-eight per cent of its area is desert or semi-desert, and although this still lags behind Australia (eighty per cent), the total of 17.3 million square kilometres of arid or semi-arid regions represents a vast amount, especially as fifteen per cent is classified as hyper-arid. Africa's leading role is due largely to the Sahara, which with an area of 9 million square kilometres is by far the biggest desert in the world, crossing the continent from the Atlantic to the Red Sea. It is the only desert in the world that constitutes a single, continuous hyper-arid belt. It is part of the Old World arid belt that begins in Mauritania, crosses North Africa and the deserts of Arabia, and reaches as far as China.

If the deserts in the Horn of Africa are included, seventy-six per cent of the Earth's surface north of the Equator is desert or semi-desert. South of the Equator, the desert along the tropic of Capricorn is not continuous, owing to the effect of the ocean currents on the tropical climate. In the Namib, the Benguela current from the Antarctic reinforces the aridity, whereas in the southeast the warm currents from the Indian Ocean reduce it. In the centre of southern Africa lie the Kalahari and the Karoo. They are not really deserts at all, because the rainfall – mostly in the summer months – has led to relatively rich vegetation. Quite clearly, the African deserts north of the Equator are far more arid than those that lie south. The reasons for this – including the high pressure over Tibet during the summer – are described in the chapter 'Types of Desert and their Causes'.

Scale: 1 cm = 300 km

# THE SAHARA DESERT

With an area of 9 million square kilometres, the Sahara is by far the biggest desert in the world. It stretches from the Atlantic in the west across more than 6,000 km to the Red Sea in the east, and from the Mediterranean coast and the southern slopes of the Atlas Mountains in the north some 2,000 km to the Sahel zone in the south. Morocco, Western Sahara, Mauritania, Mali, Algeria, Tunisia, Libya, Niger, Chad, Sudan and Egypt all have their share of it. The Sahara separates the Mediterranean world from Sub-Saharan Africa, and because of its size and its importance, geographers speak of it as a desert continent. The Sahara is a typical subtropical desert, and its climate is determined by its situation on both sides of the tropic of Cancer. In western Mauritania, another factor is its proximity to the cold Canaries current. The climate of the Sahara is extreme in all respects. The sky is mainly cloudless, the sun shines for some 4,000 hours a year, there is very little moisture in the air, and

there is almost no vegetation – all of which makes the Sahara the hottest of all the large deserts. Summer temperatures vary considerably according to the time of day, but on average they rise to over 45°C, and in the Algerian oasis of In Salah a temperature of 55°C has been recorded in the shade. As there are no clouds or vegetation, the temperature drops dramatically at night, with a variation of as much as 50°C. There is an even greater variation of temperature according to the seasons. In winter it is often no more than 15°C in the central Sahara, especially in the mountainous regions where it can fall as low as minus 20°C at night.

The cooling-off at night leads to a process of surface inversion: instead of the temperature falling with height, it increases, so that the cooler, isolated layers of air down below become stable – which is the reason why at night there is generally no wind in the Sahara. In the early hours of the morning, the air

Dunes in the Algerian erg of Admer.

223

close to the surface warms up, the inversion is swiftly dissi-pated, and the wind begins to blow again. Long before the sun has reached its zenith, the lower layers of air have warmed to such a degree that the temperature higher up falls rapidly. The hot air near the surface then rises convectively, which creates an optical impression of shimmering air. Distant objects appear closer, and the fibrous convective bands make them look like they are emerging from a sheet of water. The result is a mirage, the fata morgana that has enlivened many a book and film.

The relative air moisture reaches record levels of three to five per cent, and in many parts of the eastern central Sahara the potential annual evaporation is 6,000 mm. Any occasional, weak precipitation therefore frequently fails even to reach the ground, because it has already evaporated a few hundred metres above the surface. The minimum rainfall for plant life to be possible is 5 mm, and anything less will evaporate before the plants can absorb the water.

In all regions of the Sahara, the drying effect of the air is rein-forced by the wind, which continually brings in new dry air. Nowhere in the Sahara are there more than thirty days in the year without wind. For the most part, the winds do not cause sandstorms, and they tend to blow in the same direction and at a constant speed. The northeasterly trade wind, known in many regions as the Harmattan, has its origins in the balance between the subtropical high pressure over the Sahara and the low pressure over the Equator. The Coriolis effect, caused by the Earth's rotation, diverts it and makes it blow constantly from the north-east into the Sahara. There are also countless other local winds that blow in the different regions and seasons, and are known by names such as Khamsin, Sirocco and Gibli. In Sudan, the monsoon that brings rain to the southern Sahara is Haboob.

The dreaded sandstorms take place mainly in the hot season. A precondition for such events is a wind speed of more than 15 m per second, and according to the weight of the sand and the speed of the wind, the particles (10 g sand per cubic metre of air) are blown several metres into the air. Particles of dust can be blown up to 5,000 m high, whereas the sand stays in layers close to the ground.

In geological terms, the Sahara is a tableland 200–500 m above sea level, with wide basins and depressions, surmounted by the Hoggar Mountains and the Tibesti highlands. To the south are highlands such as the Aïr and the Adrar des Iforas. The northeastern region climbs towards the south, and in Djebel Uweinat reaches a height of almost 200 m. Further south are the Ennedi highlands. East of the Nile Valley, in the Arabian and Nubian Deserts, the land bulges upwards until it comes to a sheer drop down to the Red Sea. The crystalline underground, which becomes visible in the rises and the mountains, is over-laid with sediments such as volcanic dust, and studded with columns of basalt. Expanses of detritus-covered rock (ham-madas) are typical of the landscape, as are expanses of small stones (reg) and gravel (serir). In the wide basins, the wind has blown together detritus and masses of sand from the wadis to form dunes. Most of the basins and depressions have no drainage, and especially in the northern Sahara there are many salt marshes and salt pans. The Nile and the Niger are two per-manent rivers, with the former crossing the Sahara from south to north, while the Niger skirts round it in a wide arc.

Geographers have made many attempts to divide the Sahara into sections. A latitudinal split is one possibility, with the north Sahara lying above 25°, and the remainder of the desert classi-fied as south Sahara. There is a climatic difference between the two sections in so far as any rain that falls in the north does so during the winter months, whereas in the south it falls during the summer. The central area is also frequently referred to as the central Sahara.

Another possible division is longitudinal, into east and west on either side of 10° east. At this degree of longitude, the coast-line changes direction very abruptly, both in the north (Tunisia) and in the south (Cameroon), so that this division fits in with the structure of the continent. The eastern region is generally flatter and drier than the western, and the east – the centre of the Libyan-Egyptian Desert – is the most arid area of the Sahara.

Heinrich Schiffers, editor of one of the most comprehensive books on the Sahara, divides the desert into western, central and eastern. The western section lies between the Atlantic and the foothills of the central mountains, and consists of plateaux that rise 400 m from the coast to the east. An outstanding feature here is the massive Wasi Dra, which extends 1,200 km from the High Atlas to the Atlantic. South of the High Atlas is the Tafilalt Oasis, an area which for many Europeans is the first point of contact with the Sahara. For sheer desolation, it is hard to beat the stony serir of the Tanezrouft in southwest Algeria, where the sea of sand known as the Erg Chech stretches out to the west. Northwest of Timbuktu is the sandy El Djouf, which was first explored in the mid-1950s.

Within the western Sahara, there are no settlements with the one exception of Taoudenni, which once lay on the main caravan

A sura or chapter from the Koran, written on wood, Mali.

Children in Atbara, an important Sudanese trading centre on the Nile.

route from Morocco to Timbuktu. In the south, the western Sahara becomes a strip of semi-desert that runs from Senegal to the bend in the Niger and into the Sahel-Sudan zone.

The central Sahara is dominated by the Hoggar and the Tibesti highlands. Both are over 3,000 m high, and their valleys are full of oases. To the southwest and south of the Hoggar, surrounded by extensive tassilis (plateau landscapes), are the Adrar des Iforas and the Aïr Mountains. Between the latter and the Tibesti is the former basin of Lake Chad, now covered by the Erg du Bilma. This stretches 750 km from the Tibesti to the Aïr Mountains and covers an area of 350,000 km², with the famous Erg du Ténéré forming its northwestern part. Lake Chad takes up the remainder of what was once a colossal basin.

The northern section of the central Sahara is dominated by four large areas of dunes: the Grand Erg Occidental and the Grand Erg Oriental in Algeria, and the Idehan Awbari and the Idehan Marzuq in Libya. On the edge of these ergs are important chains of oases, such as Fezzan in Libya. The Tuat and Tidikelt oases in Algeria lie in the south of the flat Tademait Plateau.

The eastern Sahara is formed by a generally uniform plateau with several large depressions containing oases. In the south, between the Tibesti and the Nile, these are part of a gigantic sandstone plateau which is broken up by a few table mountains. Further to the north are the table mountain landscape of Kufra with its tiny isolated oases, more desolate, stony stretches of serir, the dune-covered surfaces of the Libyan sands, and the Egyptian depressions with the oases of Bahariya, Dakhla and El Kharga. Also in the north, there is another zone of depressions with a number of oases, the best known of which is Siwa.

East of the Nile Valley, in the Arabian and Nubian deserts, the land gradually rises to 2,500 m before falling steeply in the east. This region is full of valleys, and because of the relatively high rainfall is marked by steppe-like vegetation. Klaus Giessner has shown that the palaeoclimate of the Sahara for a time actually supported savanna landscapes in which both hunters and gatherers were able to live. Since the 1990s, there has been an observable increase in annual rainfall, which is not necessarily due to global warming. It seems more likely that the cause is the natural variations in rainfall that have led to the increasing number of droughts in the Sahel since the mid 1970s and 1980s (for further details on the changes in the climate of the Sahara, see Professor Giessner's published works on the subject).

In total there are some 2.5 million people living in the Sahara, mostly in the oases. The dividing line is 25° of latitude:

the 4.4 million square kilometres of the southern Sahara contain thirty-six settlements, but only 100,000 inhabitants, and half of these live in the six oases of Zouerate, Atar, Tamanrasset, Agadez, Bardaï and Arlit. The north, however, with its chain of oases, has a much higher population, particularly since the discovery of oil, which has resulted in towns such as Hassi Messaoud.

As regards ethnic distribution, there are three discernible divisions: the Arabic or Arabophone (many of the inhabitants are Berbers who speak Arabic), the Tuaregs and the Tubus. The Arabic-speaking people live in the north and west of the Tuareg region, from Egypt to the Atlantic, in the Saharan parts of Libya, Tunisia, Algeria, Morocco and Mauritania. Arabic is also spoken in a southern band that stretches from the Nile to Chad. The second group is the Tuaregs, who live in the Hoggar, Tassili n'Ajjer and Aïr Mountains, as well as on the bend of the Niger in Mali. They include the Belas, who speak the Tuareg language Tamashek. The Tubus live between Lake Chad and the Tibesti Mountains, as well as in Borku, and as far north as Kufra in Libya.

Twenty years ago, books on the Sahara used to say that sixty per cent of the inhabitants lived in oases, while the rest were nomads. The proportion of nomads has now dropped consider-ably. Many of them have settled in the oases, where they often own land or palm groves, while others have been forced by the droughts to flee to the cities of the southern Sahara countries. Nevertheless, there are still hundreds of thousands of nomads living in the Sahara, and indeed in the valleys of Ennedi, Tobestu, Aïr and Adrar des Iforas this is the only possible way of life. Together with the deserts of Central Asia, the Sahara is one of the last regions on Earth where nomadism remains the means of survival best adapted to the prevailing natural conditions – despite the efforts of successive governments to solve what they regard as the 'nomad problem' by forcing these people into settlements.

A Tuareg girl in the mountain oasis of Timia.

The group of mountains known as Mont
Gaultier lies in a remote border region between
Algeria and Niger.

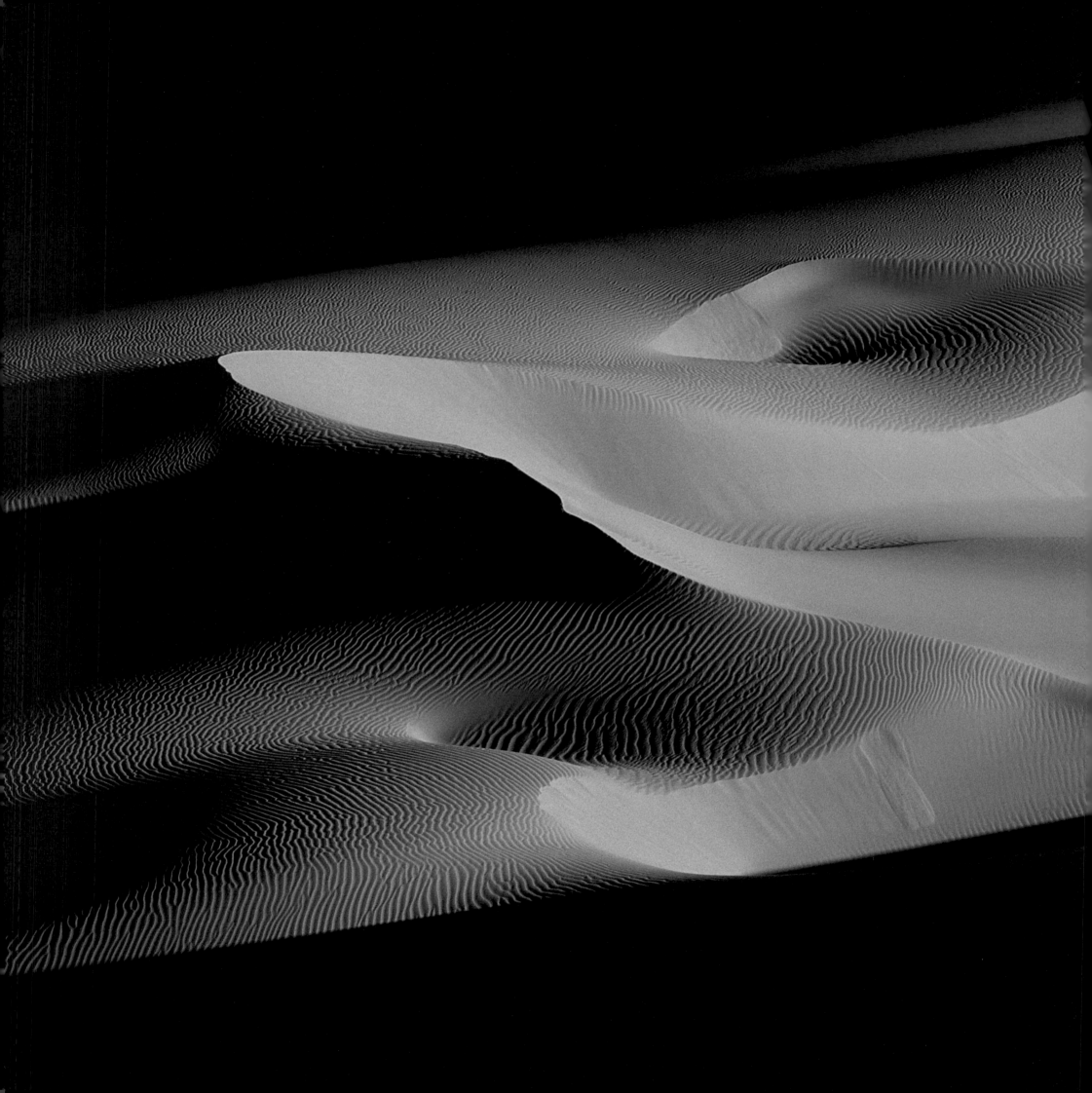

Dunes in the Arakao, the massive volcanic crater
on the eastern edge of the Aïr. Arakao means
'crab pincers', an image for the dark mountains
that surround the sea of dunes.

In the Kogo Mountains, on the eastern edge
of the Aïr highlands, are rocks of whitish blue
marble, which were formed originally under high
pressure and in blisteringly hot temperatures.

Children in the Tuareg oasis of Timia in the Aïr.

The mosque of Agadez is famous for its minaret. Constructed in Sudanese style,
the clay mosque offers a haven of quiet reflection to the faithful.

Mohamed Kamatma of Agadez is one of the
best-known silversmiths in the Sahara.
Because of their work with fire, silversmiths
are highly respected among the Tuaregs.

Every day hundreds of camels make their way through the Archi Gorge in the Ennedi Mountains. At the end is a large guelta that never runs dry, and here there are a few crocodiles, though they are now threatened with extinction.

The inhabitants of a village north of Lake Chad
seek refuge from an approaching sandstorm.
The region is notorious for its sandstorms, and
there are only about thirty days in the year when
the wind does not blow.

247

The gigantic herds of the Bororo are
undermining the fragile ecosystem of
the Sahel. However, woodcutting and
unsuitable forms of agriculture have also
contributed to desertification, which poses
the biggest environmental threat to many
countries on the southern edge of the Sahara.

The Mauritanian oasis of Chinguetti was famous in the medieval Islamic world as a centre of learning.

Precious Koranic writings and scholarly manuscripts are still preserved in the libraries.

Somewhere along the Mauritanian 'Road of Hope',

a girl flees from a sandstorm on her way home from a well.

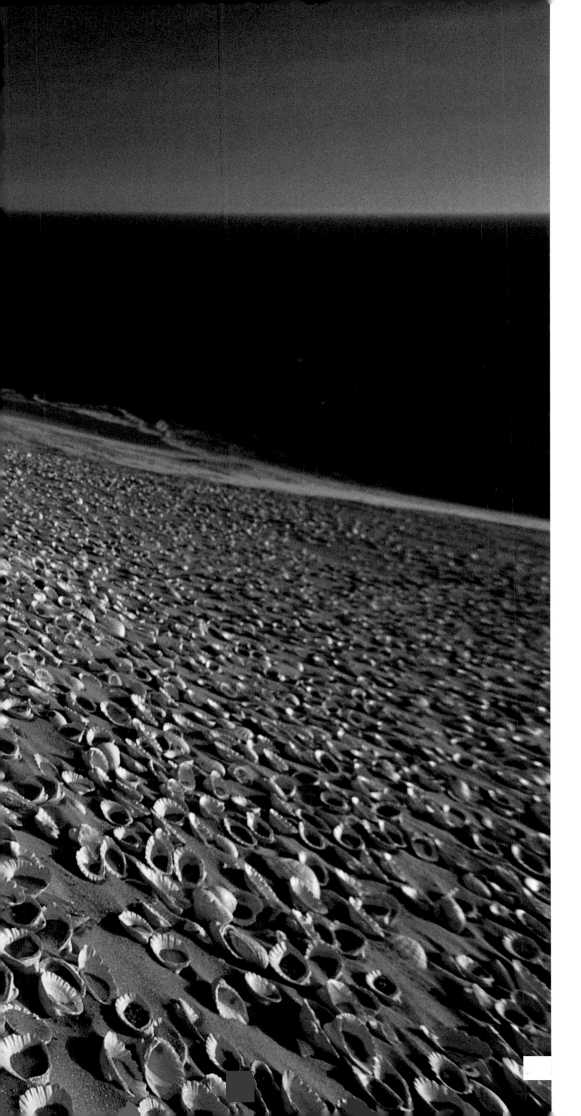

In Mauritania the Sahara goes all the way
down to the Atlantic Ocean. Far inland, the
dunes are covered with shells.

257

# DANAKIL-SOMALIA

The deserts and semi-deserts of northeastern Africa present geographers with major problems of description and delineation. For one thing, deserts, semi-deserts and thornbush savannas encroach on one another within a small area. Indeed, there is not even a unifying name. In my own book, *The Deserts of Africa*, I have used the term 'deserts of the Rift Valley', but this ignores the fact that the desert regions of the Somali peninsula are not part of the Rift Valley. Théodore Monod had considerable misgivings over his own term 'Danakil-Somalia', as it leaves out the deserts of northern Kenya. Nevertheless, my own journeys to northern Kenya, Somalia and, more recently, to the Danakil Depression have persuaded me to adopt Monod's proposal, because the Danakil is not only the biggest, but also the most extreme desert in every respect in the northeast of Africa.

The aridity of the deserts in this region has two main causes. Firstly, they are affected by the northern trade wind, which blows hot, dry air masses from the Arabian peninsula that drive away the moist Equatorial air. Secondly, the relief of the Rift Valley results in a huge difference between the rainfall on the leeward side and the much lower rainfall on the windward side. The hyper-arid Danakil Depression lies on the leeward side of the Ethiopian highlands.

Rainfall charts of northeastern Africa divide it up into three desert regions, which together make up Danakil-Somalia. The first of these regions lies between Lake Turkana and the Kenyan provincial capital of Marsabit, whose northern part is known by its local name of the Chalbi desert. Near Marsabit, the landscape is dominated by a volcanic massif which is covered with dense tropical forest. Before they were wiped out by poachers, elephants with unusually long tusks were to be found in these parts. South of the Chalbi is the Kaisut, and both of these deserts are typical nomad country.

Salt lake in the Danakil Basin.

Red Sea

ERITREA

• Massawa

Asmara •

Dallol

Erta Ale

DANAKIL

Gulf of Aden

Lake Tana

Afar-
Triangle

DJIBOUTI

Blue Nile

Berbera •

SOMALIA

• Addis Ababa

ETHIOPIA

Ogaden

Rift Valley

Lake Turkana

CHALBI-
DESERT

• Marsabit

• Mogadishu

KAISUT
DESERT

KENYA

Indian

Ocean

Lake Victoria

• Nairobi

Between the Ethiopian border and Marsabit live some 70,000 Borana. Between Marsabit and the east bank of Lake Turkana are 30,000 Gabbra, and further south are the Samburu, whose neighbours are the culturally similar Rendille. West of Lake Turkana is the land of the Turkana, who even today send war parties south into the adjacent territory of the Pokot and the Samburu. In accordance with what nature has to offer, the Samburu, Pokot, Turkana and Borana raise cattle, while the Rendille and Gabbra raise camels, but with dwindling resources cattle farmers have also gone over to camels in recent times.

Very little research has been done on the desert regions of the Somali peninsula, which are also part of Danakil-Somalia. The peninsula slopes down to the Indian Ocean from medium heights, but then rises again in places on the northern side to over 2,000 m. Off the Gulf of Aden is a typical coastal desert. The Somali peninsula takes its name from the Somali people. Many millions share the Islamic faith and feel a strong ethnic and cultural tie.

The third desert region of Danakil-Somalia is the Afar Triangle. This covers an area of 150,000 km², and is bounded in the west by the steep slopes of the Ethiopian highlands, in the east by the Red Sea, and in the south by a line from Awash to the Somali coastal town of Berbera. The northern point of this triangle is the Eritrean port of Massawa.

The Afar Triangle is one of the geologically most active regions in the world. The volcano Erta Ale, with its sea of molten lava, is visible proof of the hot stone mass seething below. A plume of melting rocks from the Earth's mantle presses against the crust, which domes and finally breaks. The cracks broaden into rifts, and these develop into volcanoes – a process that has been going on for millions of years and continues even today. In the Afar Triangle, the Earth's crust above the plume has ruptured in the form of a star. Geologists describe it as a triple point, and although it is a fairly common phenomenon on the world's seabeds, it is only at the Afar Triangle that three tectonic plates come up against one another.

In the course of the last forty million years, pressure from the interior of the Earth has opened up three rifts, which extend outwards at angles of 120°. Two of these, in the Red Sea and the Gulf of Aden, are now filled with sea water. They separate the Arabian from the African plate, and the outward movement is still in progress. Satellite surveys have shown that Africa and Arabia are drifting apart at a rate of one and a half to two centimetres a year. The third and most recent rift – the Rift Valley in

East Africa – is less active. It is widening at about six millimetres a year. It stretches for thousands of kilometres, from the Afar Triangle south through the savannas of East Africa as far as Mozambique, where it disappears into the Indian Ocean. It may well be that in a few million years, the sea will also fill up the Rift Valley. Perhaps then there will be a new ocean that splits the African continent. The starting-point of these three rifts is the Danakil Depression in the Afar Triangle.

Here too lies the volcano Erta Ale, which in the Afar language is called 'the smoking mountain'. It has two craters, one of which contains a lava lake that is unlike any other in the world. Its surface is covered with a black, metallically shining skin which is permeated with glowing red cracks. Every few minutes, fountains of lava shoot up from the lake to a height of some 15 m. After one or two minutes, the fountain collapses back into the melt, creating a kind of whirlpool that sucks down large sections of the lake's skin.

Seventy-five km further north, 120 m below sea level, is the Dallol. Hot bubbling springs spew salt out of the Earth, and the resultant deposits produce a surreal world of vivid colours. All around the springs are massive, dazzlingly white stacks, some of them several metres high, and these in turn are surrounded by bright yellow crusts – older deposits in the depths of which are pools of clear, garish green water. Each spring bubbles for just a few weeks. The old salt deposits dry out, become pale, or turn into a rust-brown crust. The springs are situated at the lowest point of the Danakil Depression, and geologists think that the Red Sea may have penetrated into the Afar Triangle millions of years ago and vaporized, leaving the salt behind. The layer of salt in the Dallol is believed to be more than 1,000 m thick.

The Danakil desert is home to about 100,000 Afar nomads. In all, 750,000 Afars live in Ethiopia, Eritrea and Djibouti.

The volcano Erta Ale.

The lava lake of Erta Ale is the only one of its kind on Earth.

Glowing red cracks are constantly appearing, and jets of lava rise 15 m high.

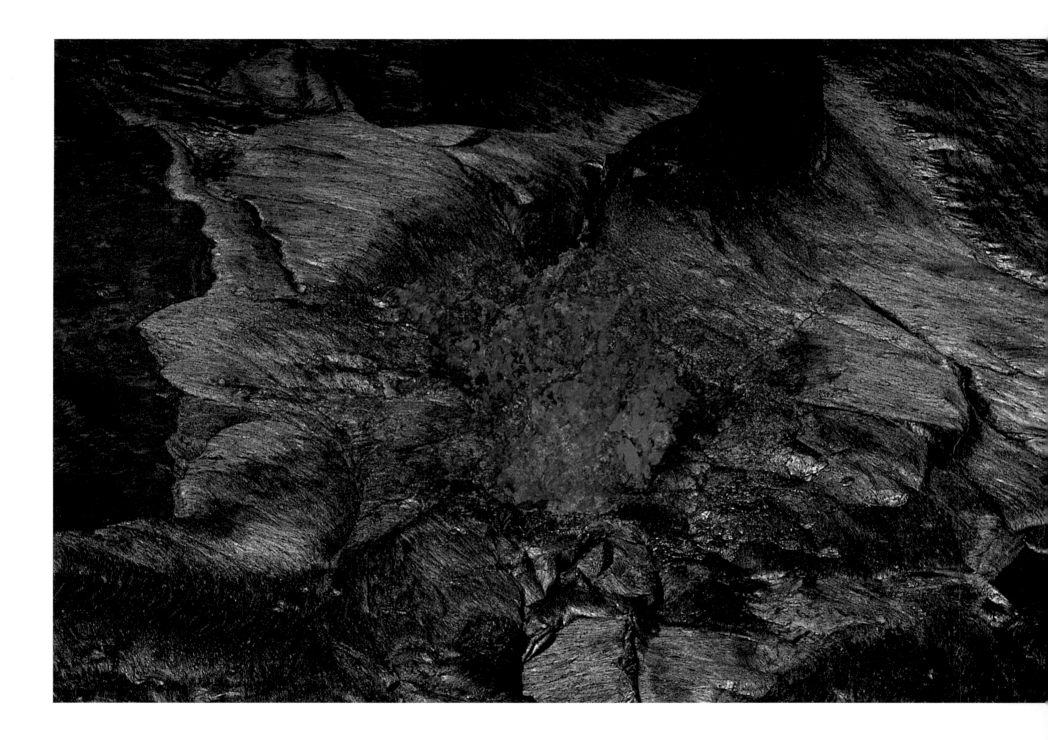

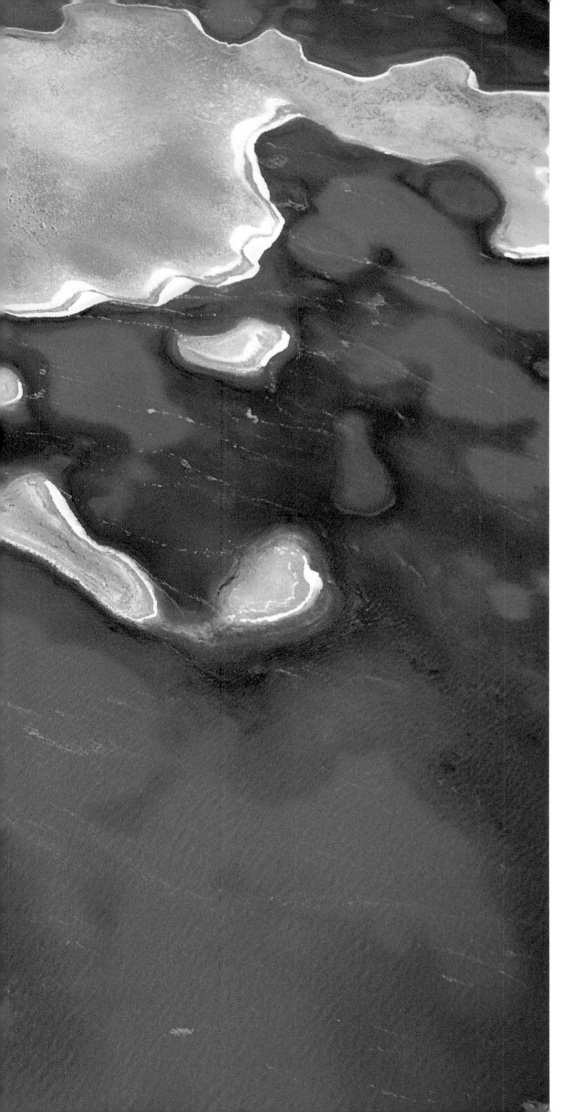

Lake Afrera, a salt lake, lies 100 m below sea level in the Danakil Basin. Algae give it a dark green colour. Aerial photo from 20 m.

In the Dallol region of the Danakil desert, ferric oxide has turned a salt lake to a reddish orange. Aerial photo from 100 m.

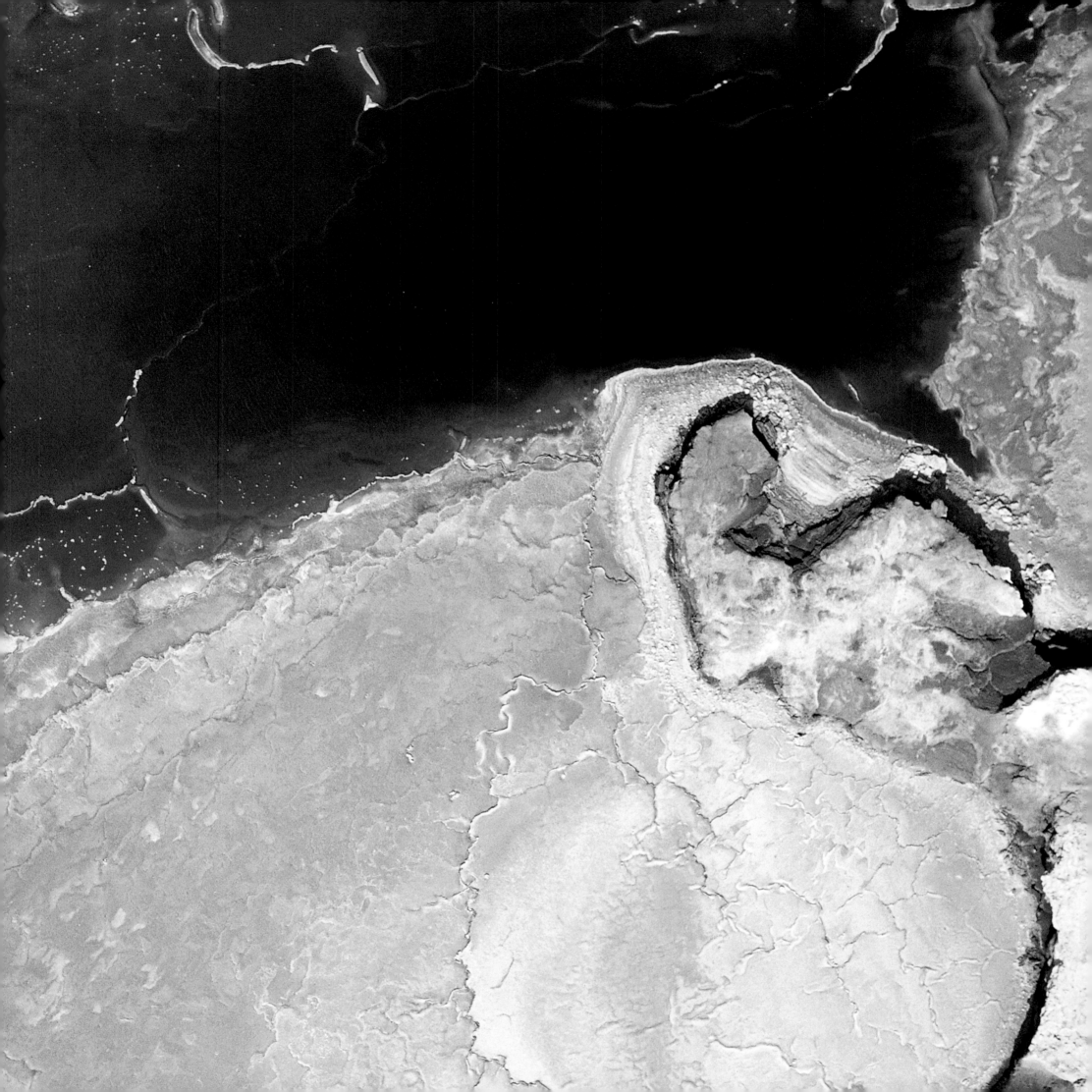

Erta Ale and its neighbouring volcanoes testify
to the tectonic movements in the Afar Triangle,
which are unique worldwide.

The Dallol lies 120 m below sea level in the north of the barely accessible Danakil Basin.

Hot springs deposit salt which takes on the colours of various minerals,

and clear green water collects in the salt crusts.

# THE KALAHARI DESERT
# AND THE KAROO DESERT

KALAHARI  The Kalahari lies in the centre of the South African subcontinent, and covers an area of 1.2 million square kilometres, which is almost five times the size of the UK. Its red sands extend from the Orange River in South Africa to the border of the Congolese rain forest, but its heart is in eastern Namibia and Botswana. Geologically, the Kalahari is one of Africa's three biggest basins.

Between 208 and 144 million years ago, the super-continent of Gondwanaland in the southern hemisphere began to break up, eventually giving birth to South America, Africa, Australia and Antarctica. One hundred million years ago, Africa itself became a continent, and shortly afterwards large areas of it were pushed upwards. At the same time, the Chad Basin in the north, the Congo Basin in central Africa, and the Kalahari Basin in the south were formed. During the next sixty million years, the highlands eroded continually, as a result of which the Kalahari

Basin was filled with sand which reached up to 300 m in thickness. Only in a few places, such as the Tsodilo Hills and the Aha Hills, can one see the rocky substructure protruding from under the masses of sand. The Kalahari Basin is divided up into smaller basins called pans. Sometimes these may contain lakes.

The Kalahari is not really a desert in the proper sense of the word. Many areas could be called semi-desert, but most of it is thornbush or arid savanna, covered with acacias or, in the north, even with forests of mopane. The annual rainfall is between 150 and 250 mm, and in the north up to 500 mm, which is anything but desert-like. The lack of surface water – caused by the extreme permeability of the sand, which leads to rapid seepage of the often heavy rainfall in the summer – may be what has led some people to call the Kalahari a desert. Only in the many pans does the water remain for some time. The best-known pans in the Kalahari include the Nxai Pan and Deception Pan.

A baobab in the Makgadikgadi salt pan.

Okavango
Delta

Tsodilo
Hills

• Maun

Makgadikgadi
Pans

• Orapa

NAMIBIA

BOTSWANA

KALAHARI

• Letlhakane

Jwaneng •

• Gaborone

SOUTH AFRICA

NAMAQUA-
LAND

GREAT KAROO

Atlantic

LITTLE KAROO

Cape
Town

Indian

Ocean

The densest population of animals in the Kalahari, if not in the whole of Africa, is to be found in the Okavango Delta. The Okavango River comes from the rain-rich Benguela Plateau in Angola, and flows for hundreds of kilometres through the Kalahari until it reaches northwestern Botswana, where it discharges itself into a huge delta which, with a length of 200 km and an area of 17,000 km², is only slightly smaller than the Nile Delta. The waters of the Okavango take five months to make their way from their source in Angola through the sands of the Kalahari to the delta at Maun, which they then proceed to flood. The absence or insufficiency of rain in Angola, together with overuse of the water for irrigation projects in Namibia, has led to a drastic lowering of the water level in the Okavango Delta and is a major threat to this unique ecosystem.

Just fifty years ago, much of the Kalahari was unexplored and inaccessible, but today it is marked out with a dense network of roads, tracks and cattle fences. Botswana was one of the ten poorest countries in the world when, in 1967, huge deposits of diamonds were discovered there. The mines of Orapa, Jwaneng and Letlhakane have made Botswana into the world's biggest diamond producer. The most important sector of the economy, however, is cattle farming. In recent years, rich owners have penetrated deeper and deeper into the Kalahari, drilling wells and thus opening up new pasture land for the eighty million head of cattle that are now there. This massive overgrazing has led to widespread destruction of the Kalahari ecosystem.

The San demonstrated impressively how one can live for thousands of years in the Kalahari without wreaking such havoc. Their hunter-gatherer way of life was totally attuned to nature. They had highly specialized knowledge of their environment, kept it properly balanced, and adapted themselves to its demands. The hunters knew of fifty-five species of edible mammals, birds, reptiles and insects, and in their search for food they would travel up to 4,000 km across the Kalahari.

KAROO    The Karoo in southwest South Africa is no more a desert than the Kalahari. It is an arid region that stretches out between the Cape Province with its winter rain and the Kalahari with its summer rain. The Little Karoo has an annual rainfall of 150–300 mm, while the Great Karoo has 125–200 mm. North of the Karoo is the Namaqualand, which also receives just 50–200 mm of rain a year, and whose northern section extends beyond the Orange River into Namibia. The Karoo and the Namaqualand are covered with bushes and shrubs, and, after rainfall, large areas are also filled with bright flowers.

Scale: 1 cm = 75 km

Quivertrees on the western edge of the Kalahari. The trunk and branches
are easy to hollow out, and the San used to make their arrows with them.

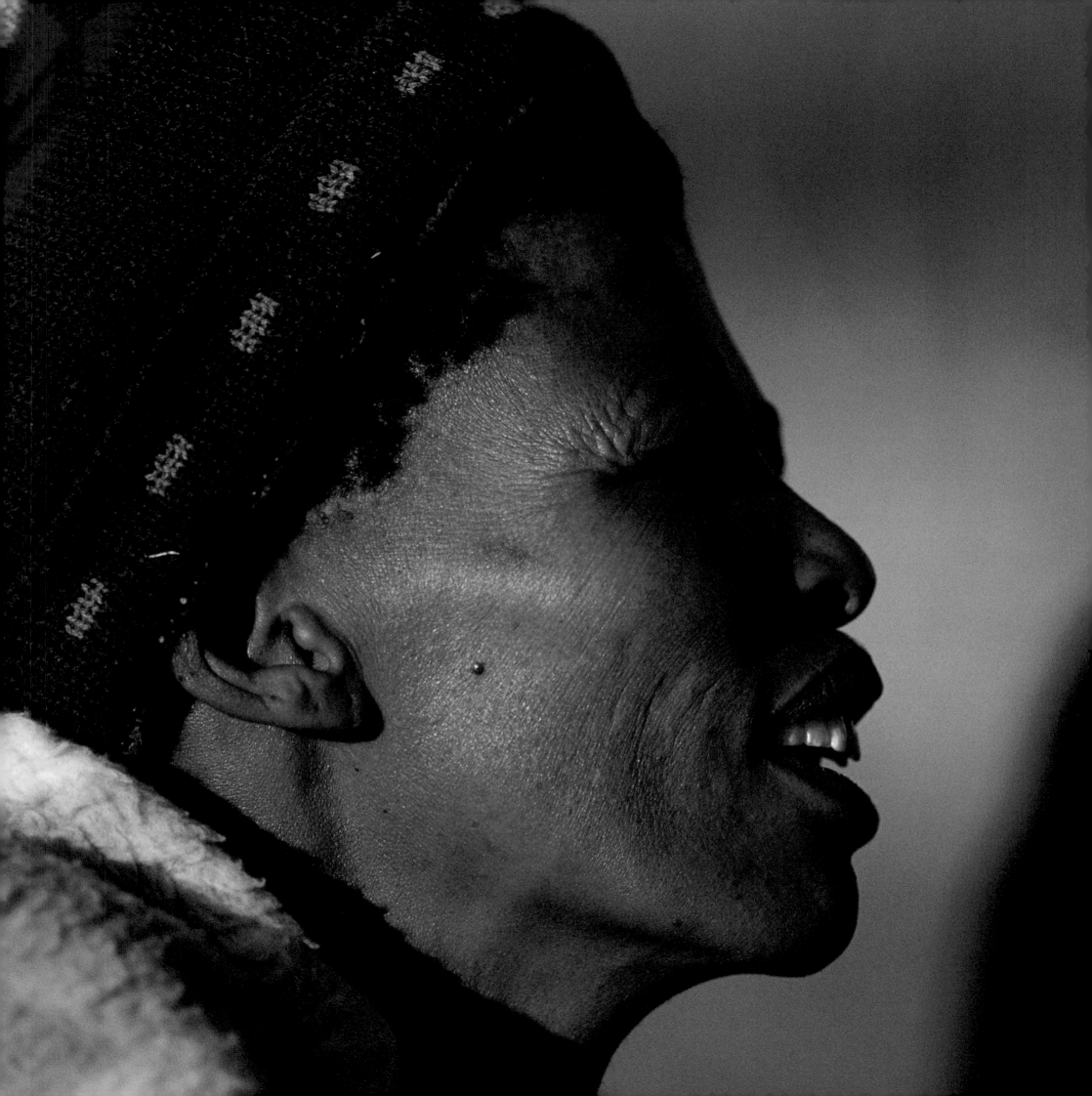

Unlike their ancestors before them, who roamed the Kalahari for 30,000 years,

the San no longer live as hunter-gatherers.

Salt pans like the Makgadikgadi are typical
of the Kalahari, many areas of which can
scarcely be called desert country.

282

# THE NAMIB DESERT

By comparison with the Sahara, the Namib is a tiny desert. It is 2,000 km long and 30–100 km wide, with an area of just 270,000 km². Its southern boundary is the Orange River, and to the north it extends into Angola; the western boundary is the Atlantic, and the eastern the Great Escarpment that runs the length of Namibia from north to south. From here it slopes from 800 m down to sea level.

Although the Namib is often described as a typical coastal desert, its aridity is due partly to its situation on both sides of the tropic of Capricorn. The lack of rain is exacerbated by its close proximity to a cold ocean current. While the Sahara follows the tropic of Cancer for more than 6,000 km from the Atlantic to the Red Sea, the Namib follows the tropic of Capricorn for only 30–100 km from the Atlantic into the African mainland. The reason for this is the powerful ocean currents that change the effects of atmospheric circulation in southern Africa and prevent a continual band of desert from the Atlantic to the Indian Ocean. On the Atlantic Coast, however, the Benguela current coming from the Antarctic exacerbates the aridity of the tropic. The ice-cold water cools the air masses above the ocean, and when they reach the mainland, an inversion takes place between the warmer, dry air masses above it and the lower, cooler, moist air, which prevents the convection necessary for the substantial production of rain. Near the coast, however, a fog forms which is driven inland by the powerful ocean winds. This fog often lasts all day, but does not penetrate any further than 30 km inland. The extent of the fog is also the decisive factor in distinguishing between the coastal and inner Namib, the latter of which is linked to the 'pre-Namib'.

The nearer it comes to the coast, the less rain it receives. Almost every morning a wall of fog settles over it, caused by the rapid cooling at night of the ocean air which has moved in during

Himba nomads in the Kaokoveld.

ANGOLA

Kunene

Kaokoveld

NAMIBIA

Cape Cross

Swakopmund●  ● Windhoek

Atlantic

Kuiseb

Sossusvlei

N
A
M
I
B
D
E
S
E
R
T

Lüderitz ●

Orange River

SOUTH AFRICA

the day; the fog only lifts late in the morning, if it lifts at all. It is the equivalent to a yearly rainfall of 40–50 mm, and this is what provides a basis for the flora of the coastal Namib, whose best-known plant is the Welwitschia mirabilis. With its two leathery leaves, a metre long, this plant – which is often hundreds of years old – sucks in the moisture from the fog and thus makes itself independent of groundwater and rain. The botanist Friedrich Welwitsch (1806–72) was the first to describe this evolutionary curiosity in 1860.

The coast of the Namib is also home to millions of seabirds and seals. The reason for this is the Benguela current, which contains an extraordinary amount of oxygen and plankton, making these coastal waters the richest place on Earth for fish. These in their turn feed the cormorants and seals, of which there is a colony of some 200,000 at Cape Cross. On some of the islands off Lüderitz Bay there are even colonies of penguins – a reminder that the Benguela current begins in the Antarctic. There are, however, far fewer species of fauna along the coast than in the inner Namib or the pre-Namib. Along the dry valleys there are even lions.

East of the coastal strip, which measures between 30 and 50 km in width, lies the inner Namib. At a height of 400–500 m, it is beyond the reach of the coastal fog and, with the resultant high temperatures and lack of moisture, it comes closest to the general concept of a desert climate.

The pre-Namib at the foot of the Great Escarpment receives an annual rainfall of 100 mm, which allows for large-scale cattle farming. To the north is the western section of the Kaokoveld, where the nomadic Himbas live. In the south, farmers run huge farms of cattle and karakul sheep at the foot of the Rand, which here rises to 1,800 m. The vegetation is so sparse that a single cow needs a grazing area of 30 hectares, and the extremely erratic precipitation is a constant source of problems. At the beginning of the 1980s, the Himbas lost almost all their cattle as a result of drought, and the lack of rain in the 1990s forced many farmers in the east of the Namib to sell their livestock. The few settlements that are left in the Namib are either on the eastern side or on the coast, and the inner Namib is uninhabited.

The climatic pattern of the coastal, inner and pre-Namib follows the north-south line of the coast. There are also clear geomorphological divisions: north of the Kuiseb, a dry river, are flat deserts of stone and gravel that are furrowed by the dry riverbeds of the Hoanib, Hoarusib and Ugab. South of the Kuiseb are the Namib dunes, which often rise to a height of

300 m and go as far as the Orange. The Kuiseb very seldom reaches the Atlantic, but there are enough occasions when it fills with water to prevent the dunes from moving northwards.

The dune region is also crisscrossed by dry riverbeds, though these are generally covered by the sand and form clay pans that are known as *vleis*. The Tsauchab reaches furthest into the dune region, and its course is marked by centuries-old camel thorns. It very rarely has any water in it, and even more rarely is there enough to reach as far as the Sossusvlei. In 1997, however, after a gap of many years, this miracle of nature occurred once again, and it has been repeated several times since. In the midst of the lofty dunes, there suddenly appears a lake which, as if by magic, attracts hordes of antelope, flamingos and, above all, tourists.

The Namib is often called the oldest desert in the world. The alternating historical phases of wet and dry that have characterized the Sahara, for instance, scarcely seem to have applied to the Namib. The reason for this is the Benguela current, which for ten million years has ensured a continuous lack of rain. The Benguela current originated in the Tertiary Period, when Antarctica drifted close to the pole, and the South Atlantic opened up. The extraordinary length of time that these desert conditions have existed explains why the fauna of the Namib are unusually specialized. On the other hand, the existence of the Welwitschia in the extremely arid environment of today is regarded by geographers as evidence that even in the Namib there must once have been phases moist enough to allow this plant to evolve.

In the south of the Namib are the biggest and purest diamonds on Earth, and they remain the most important element of the Namibian economy. The discovery of these precious stones was made by a German railway official named August Stauch, who in April 1908 saw a nondescript stone sticking to the shovel of one of the railway workers, and recognized its value. Before the year was over, Stauch's workers, armed with jam jars and scrabbling about on their knees, had picked 39,000 carats of rough diamonds out of the sand and had made Stauch a millionaire.

Kolmanskop, east of Lüderitz, became a diamond town, with post office, swimming pool, slaughterhouse and school. Before the First World War, German mining companies were producing a fifth of the world's diamonds, but in the 1920s the diamond rush switched to the southern edge of the Namib. There, in a hermetically sealed-off no-go area 322 km by 96 km, 200 kg of rough diamonds are produced every year. In the meantime, Kolmanskop has become a ghost town.

Evening, and a Himba boy drives his herd of goats into the fold.

Nomadic livestock farming is the basic occupation of the Himba people

in the Kaokoveld, on the eastern edge of the Namib.

In spite of droughts and war, the Himba have managed to maintain

their traditional nomadic way of life.

294

Residents of the village of Purros in the Kaokoveld. Many people have
left the village and have moved to the Namibian capital Windhoek.

Aerial photo of dunes in the Namib.

The southern part of the Namib is covered with dunes of many

different shapes and colours. Aerial photo from 400 m.

The Dead Vlei is a clay pan which is separated
by a dune from the famous Sossusvlei.
This is why it gets no water when, a few times
every hundred years, the Tsauchab flows into
the Sossusvlei.

# DESERTS OF THE EARTH

Desert Landscapes

# THE PROCESSES THAT FORM DESERT LANDSCAPES

According to popular belief, many deserts are dried-up oceans. The salt lakes and seas of sand may have contributed to this idea, as have the oceanic dimensions of many deserts, and indeed there are some that do lie in regions that were once seas, such as the Aral-Caspian Depression. The Kara-Kum and Kyzyl-Kum deserts which now fill this gigantic basin do not, however, have anything to do with the fact that it was once covered by a sea. The present form of the landscape is due mainly to the effects of weathering and erosion. In the discussions of the latter in the course of this chapter, it is important to bear in mind that the overall relief of the deserts did not originate under conditions of aridity. Cuestas, the great dry valleys, and even the ergs are what we call ancient forms, which go back to wetter or windier times and later became fixed. It is, however, sometimes difficult to distinguish between current processes, and those that have long since ceased but have left their permanent mark on the landscape.

To clarify, let us begin with the terms 'weathering' and 'erosion'. Under the influence of external forces, solid rock on the Earth's surface is slowly but steadily loosened, worked on and broken down. This is the process we call weathering. Erosion, on the other hand, is caused by a number of individual processes that may be separated by time and place or intensity but are all connected with gravity. Prime causes include running water, the wind and glaciers. There is a distinction here between erosion, which is a linear process, and denudation. The latter involves the removal of surface materials, which may occur in a variety of ways. In deserts it is the wind that plays a decisive role.

Meanwhile, there are two basic forms of weathering: mechanical and chemical. Mechanical weathering leads to the destruction of the rock without changing its mineral

The Arabic word *erg* means a sea of dunes, no matter how big.

In the eastern Sahara, the Tuareg term *edyen* is also in common use.

The equivalent in Arabia is *nafud*, and in Central Asia *kum*.

Rocks on the edge of the Namib.

Rock formations in Tagrera, Algeria.

components. Chemical weathering, however, dissolves the water-soluble minerals or transforms those that are water-insoluble into soluble substances. As there is no water in deserts, the latter process is far less common than the former, but it does still play a part.

One form of mechanical weathering is insolation weathering, also known as thermoclasty. In deserts there are often huge differences between day and night temperatures, and these can lead to alternating expansion and contraction, which loosens the minerals and gradually breaks down the rocks. Saline weathering depends on an increasing volume of salts, and it occurs through thermal expansion, the growth of crystals, and hydration. The latter is a mixed form of mechanical and chemical weathering, and often occurs in coastal deserts because of the high degree of moisture in the air. Crystallizing salts cause decomposition in the structure of the rock. In the desert, the salts absorb any moisture and occasional rain and turn into hydrates, as a result of which they may expand in volume by 30–100 per cent. Many of the phenomena that used to be attributed to insolation weathering are in fact probably due to saline weathering, which may even cause massive rock splits.

In regions that are not excessively arid, there is a very special form of weathering known as desquamation or exfoliation. Extreme changes in temperature by day and by night cause the outer rock layers to peel, shedding flakes whose size may vary from millimetres to centimetres. The latest research has shown that there are also micro-organisms at work here. When granite domes shed metre-thick layers that run parallel to the surface, the cause is quite different: pressure is released when the material that lies on top of them is eroded.

In deserts one can often see rock surfaces with hollows. These are called tafoni, and they are caused by shade weathering: in the shade, the moisture lasts longer and leads to more intensive chemical weathering, and hence to a hollowing process. This has its own dynamic, because the further the tafoni penetrate into the rock, the larger the area of shade.

Desert varnish, a common sight in arid zones, is the result of chemical weathering, which works outwards from the interior of the rock and is therefore known as nuclear weathering. A coating of manganese oxide, iron oxide or silicic acid is drawn to the surface, and the wind polishes it into a shining film.

Karst landforms (full of surface hollows) are usually associated with more moderate climates, but they are also found in deserts. The process occurs microscopically through the fall of dew. Karst occurs in rocks that do not contain limestone, and it often creates spectacular landscapes such as the Tassili du Hoggar in southern Algeria.

'Erosion', a process in which the surface is worn away, is sometimes used rather loosely. Yet, it has played and still plays a major role in shaping the desert landscape both in earlier, wetter times and today. The great valley systems of the deserts took on their current appearance – even if they already existed during earlier periods – mainly in the Tertiary and Pleistocene epochs. The changes now are minimal, and are caused by episodic rainfall. In regions where the winds are strong and the sand accumulates in large quantities, however, it can happen at any time that these valleys might be completely buried in sand. Satellite pictures have shown that the lower reaches of the famous Wadi Howar – a riverbed that has some similarities with the Nile – was smothered over a distance of some 400 km. If there is any precipitation today in the arid regions, it generally comes in the form of heavy rainfall. The lack of vegetation, and the crusted or stony surfaces result in most of the rain flowing away instead of being absorbed. The wadis quickly fill up with water, which flows in torrents and causes a great deal of erosion. As a result, the effects of erosion are often far more dramatic than those caused by the wind.

Aeolian or wind erosion nevertheless plays an important role in the formation of the desert landscape, above all because there is so little vegetation on the surface. There are three ways in which wind erosion may occur: deflation, corrasion and accumulation. All three processes go together, because the wind will pick up a grain of sand but will also put it down again. The nature of accumulation will be dealt with in the next chapter.

Deflation is the process by which the wind blows unconsolidated material, and it has a major influence on the shaping of arid landscapes. This material has been loosened by weathering, and its removal may cause deflation hollows, as well as the bare-rock plateaux known as hammadas and the stony, gravel-covered serirs. With the fine materials that it gathers up, the wind can polish the rock, using the bigger grains much like a sandblaster.

The Tuaregs say that more people drown in the desert than die of thirst. The yearly rainfall arrives in the form of occasional cloudbursts, and the lack of vegetation means that the ground cannot absorb the water. The dried-up wadis then turn into raging torrents. The most famous victim of one such flash flood was the explorer Isabelle Eberhardt, who in 1904 was in her house on the edge of a wadi when it was swept away.

Corrasion (a mechanical process, as opposed to corrosion, which is a chemical process) has its optimum effect a few tens of centimetres above the ground, most strikingly in the form of mushroom rocks. Corrasion also leads to ventifacts – stones with one, two or three facets, known as einkanter, zweikanter, dreikanter, which provide evidence of the strength of the wind. The most spectacular landscape forms resulting from this process are yardangs. The word is Uygurian, and describes a crested linear ridge of rock that is broad and rounded on the windward side and sharp and narrow on the leeward side. Yardangs can vary from a few centimetres to the size of a house. The average ratio of length to breadth is four to one, in conformity with the laws that govern the mechanics of currents. Fields of yardangs are known in Iran as Shar Lut, or 'desert towns'.

Between deflation or corrasion and accumulation is the transportation of the sand by the wind. There are three different forms of transport: suspension, reptation and saltation. In the deflation process, the finest materials are suspended as dust (the borderline between sand and dust is a grain diameter of $\frac{1}{16}$ mm), which can remain in the atmosphere for a long time and be transported over long distances. Sahara dust can travel as far as Europe and even North America. If dust falls in arid regions, it will be blown away again. Only if prevented by moisture or vegetation will it turn into a sediment or deposit. This is why the great loess landscapes are to be found on the edges of arid regions. In China, loess deposits may measure up to 1,200 m in thickness. As the current rate of sedimentation is 1.2 mm a year, it must have taken a good million years for such deposits to have formed.

If coarse material is moved during the process of deflation, it rolls along the ground, and this is called reptation. The third mode, saltation, entails grains of sand jumping or bouncing, and this is the only form of transport that can lead to a build-up of major accumulations – namely, dunes – and is therefore regarded as the most important. This accumulation takes place when the wind is no longer strong enough to drive the sand onwards by way of saltation or reptation. Wind ripples are the smallest forms of accumulation, and they cover sandy surfaces that are caressed by gentler, more constant winds. The lengths of these ripples may be between a few centimetres and 5 m, while the height may rise to some 50 cm. Here the

Mushroom rocks in the Atacama, South America.

decisive form of transport is reptation. When these waves accumulate to between 5 m and 500 m in length, they are called dunes, and what they all have in common is that the sand piles up on the leeward side, forming an angle of 30°.

It may surprise some readers to learn that when it comes to the formation of desert landscapes in the present, the wind plays a secondary role to that of water. It is primarily water that causes such fundamental processes as erosion, the loosening and transport of materials, and the formation of valleys. The wind adds the finishing touches, however, by sculpting the surface through deflation, corrasion and accumulation.

Dunes in a tassili in the Hoggar Mountains, Algeria, Africa.

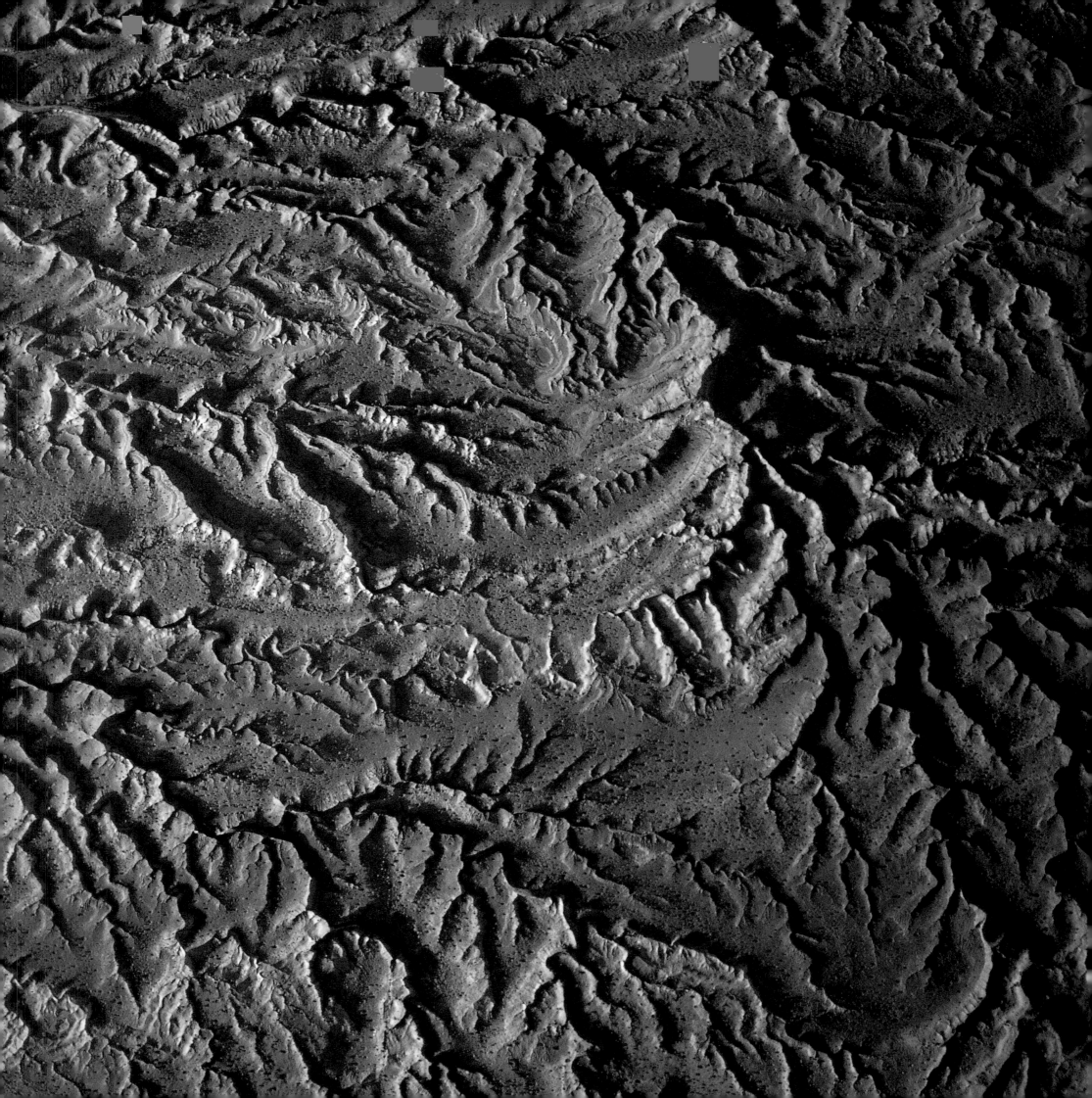

# FORMS OF DESERT LANDSCAPES

In this chapter, we shall discuss the different forms of landscapes that are characteristic of deserts. They extend far beyond the hackneyed image of endless seas of sand, even if the most spectacular landscapes remain those of the great dunes.

PIEDMONTS  The piedmont form is common to many deserts. It surrounds all the higher areas of the relief, including mountain ranges, and constitutes a link between the mountains and the plains. It is the piedmont that creates a balance between the higher and lower parts of the desert relief – a balance that is brought about by the various processes of erosion. It consists of an upper pediment, which is free from debris, and a lower glacis, which is filled with masses of detritus. Deserts with basin structures are naturally full of such areas, including the inland basin in the Iranian highlands. In the central Sahara, the areas around the central mountains are typical examples of piedmont landscapes, as are those at the foot of the Andes in the Atacama desert.

CUESTAS  These are strata of flat rock with differing degrees of resistance. They are widespread in deserts, which often contain large areas of sediment where some layers may be easily displaced by tectonic movements. Most cuestas were formed after tectonic activity during the Tertiary epoch, and in the Pleistocene epoch they took on a more permanent shape. At the bottom of these cuestas there are often depressions which have become the site of important oases – for instance in Bilma, where the cuesta stretches for 150 km from north to south, and contains the Kaouar Oases. Sometimes these strata may be completely covered by sand masses, but when the horizontal strata are undisturbed, they may give rise to stratified tablelands with mesas (table mountains) or zeugen. The latter are the remains of abraded strata that have been preserved at a greater or lesser distance from the main cuesta.

Eroded landscape on the Colorado Plateau, USA.

The table mountains and zeugen of Monument Valley are famous all over the world. This desert plain is situated in the Navajo reservation on the border between Arizona and Utah. Wind and water have eroded the soft stone and built up sandstone towers and spires that can reach as high as 30 m. Countless westerns have been filmed in this cuesta landscape.

INSELBERGS  Inselbergs (literally, island mountains) are isolated, steep-sided hills of rock that generally rise sharply out of a peneplain. They may consist of the same rock as their surroundings (a genuine inselberg) or of different structural forms (monadnocks). Along with valley systems, the inselbergs are among the most striking features of arid regions, but they too derive from wetter times.

DRY VALLEYS  The dry valleys that we see today were formed during the late Tertiary and the Pleistocene epochs. After rainfall, however, they are still subject to a degree of change. They originated in mountain ranges and cuestas. Their highest catchment areas are subject to erosion, while down in the piedmonts and foothills there is an accumulation of transported materials. The finer of these will move on into the depressions, which will be filled with such deposits. In just a few cases, the dry valleys discharge themselves into oceans, but for the most part drainage is endorheic (i.e. the flow is inward, towards the basins within the various deserts). The typical dry valley is shaped rather like a baking tin. The name given to it varies according to the region: in the Sahara and Arabian deserts it is called a wadi or *qued*, in parts of the Sahel a *kori*, in Namibia a *reviere*, and in the USA a wash.

DEPRESSIONS AND PANS  The frequency of depressions and pans in the desert arises out of a hydrographic system in which there is no access to the sea, and drainage can therefore only take place through a series of enclosed basins. There are various classifications of depressions and pans, according to the proportion of surface drainage and groundwater supply as well as the composition of the surface. There are clay pans and salt pans, neither of which has any form of drainage. The Arabic word sebhka is often used by geographers to describe these pans, but they are known by various local names: in the Maghreb they are called *schotts*, in the rest of the Sahara *sebhkas*, in Asia *kavirs* and *takyrs*, in southern Africa *vleis* or pans, in USA playas, bolsons or sinks, in South America *salars* or *salinas*, and in Australia lakes.

SERIR AND REG  This form of landscape is called reg in the western Sahara and serir in the central Sahara, especially in the Libyan Desert. German desert experts such as Wolfgang Meckelein argue that the two concepts are not identical. The reg surfaces of the western Sahara are extended plains covered with sand and gravel, whereas serir surfaces refer

For centuries, salt has been extracted from the Taoudenni sabkha in the north of Mali. Blocks are cut out of the salt deposits, split into 40 kg slabs, taken south by caravan, and sold there in the markets. In former times, salt was a precious commodity in trans-Saharan trade, and the people of the savanna and forest regions used to pay for it in gold.

especially to the vast, sediment-filled foothill plains of the central Saharan massif. Geographers from elsewhere, however, make no distinction, and tend to use the term reg. Serir is a Berber word for a gravel surface that has no vegetation, large stones or variety in its appearance. The pebbles, mostly quartz and quartzite, have been rounded by centuries of fluvial transport. They come from the great Tertiary and Pleistocene river systems, and are therefore very old forms. The typical serir of today has come about through deflation, under conditions of extreme aridity. Corrasion also occurs on these serir surfaces, with ventifacts faceted by the wind.

HAMMADAS  Hammada is an Arabic word that refers to a flat, bare-rock plateau. Monod says that hammadas are only to be found on mountain plateaux, but other geographers argue that they are independent of the relief. Meckelein divides them into limestone, sandstone and basalt hammadas, which vary in colour and size. Although the plateaux themselves are very old, the surface of the hammada is the product of arid morphodynamics (relief formation). Processes of frost weathering and saline splitting are predominant here. Hammadas are the most widespread form of desert landscape.

DUNES AND ERGS  Many people imagine all deserts to be an endless sea of sand, but in fact such dune or erg landscapes are only one of many types. Even in the Sahara they only make up twenty per cent of the area. Hardly any dunes are found outside the arid regions, and yet they remain a typical feature of the desert. Anyone flying over an erg will inevitably wonder where all the sand came from. The Libyan Desert, for instance, covers an area of 65,000 km$^2$ and contains 1,000 km$^3$ of sand. In 1909, the German geographer Albrecht Penck (1858–1945) was struck by something: vast areas of dunes are situated in basins which are frequently in close proximity to river systems. And, indeed, this is the case. The fluvial origin of the sands of the Takla Makan is incontrovertible, because the spectrum of heavy metals varies according to the different catchment areas of the rivers. Even those rivers that drain into the sea are often sources of sand, as their deposits may be blown away at low tide. Of the 100 tonnes of sediment that the Orange transports annually from South Africa to the Atlantic, 25–50 per cent consists of sand, some of which is aeolian Namib sand. Large quantities may also come

A gorge in the Negev desert in Israel.

Dunes in Arakao, Niger.

Landscape near Mont Gaultier, Algeria.

directly from the decomposition or weathering of sandstone breaking down into suitably sized grains. The wind uses the sand that is available in order to form dunes, but it does not produce the sand itself.

There is an important distinction between dunes and ergs. The former are mounds or ridges of sand that are still being shaped today, whereas the great ergs consist of draas. These are ancient forms that arose in earlier times at much higher wind speeds, but are fixed and incapable of further development. One can, however, find dunes on the draas.

The geographer Helga Besler, who specializes in the study of dunes, distinguishes between bound, free and complex types. Bound dunes arise from obstacles. They are fashioned as parallels on the leeward side of deflation hollows, when the wind-blown sand is caught up by the vegetation on the periphery. Large bushes can catch the sand, which may build up on the leeward and the windward side as well as in the bush itself. Sand-friendly plants sink their roots into the grains and can grow quite tall, thus giving rise to nebkhas (small, arrow-shaped hummocks). Leeward dunes are formed behind nebkhas or hills. The flow of sand forks on the windward side, and on the leeward side the currents meet at an angle, so that there is often a body of sand that is several kilometres long, with a crest or ridge in the middle.

Free dunes accumulate even without obstacles. They begin as little humps on the leeward side of surface waves, and as soon as they have reached a height of a few decimetres, a slope begins to form on the leeward side; then between the leeward and windward slopes, at right angles to the direction of transportation, a sharp crest is formed. The sand is driven up the windward slope, at an angle of 10–15°, by saltation and then deposited directly behind the crest – until it slides down again on the leeward side. Thus the whole mass is constantly changing its form, and as the changes are more rapid around the flat edges than at the top, small but ever-lengthening horns are formed in the direction of the movement. This gives rise to the typical crescent shape of barchans or sickle dunes. Barchans are the only true nomadic dunes, as the whole mass of sand is constantly in motion. If the wind direction is constant, and the subsoil is stable and without vegetation, barchans can shift about 30 cm in a day. The axis is always the direction of transportation.

Not so much is known about the origins of seif dunes – which are free and longitudinal – or the currents that form them. A seif is an isolated dune with a knife-edged ridge, which runs parallel to the direction of the prevailing wind. Seif is an Arabic word meaning scimitar, and as the name indicates, the ridge is slightly curved. Seif dunes are found in regions where there are two winds that generally change with the seasons. Complex dunes are a combination of barchans and seifs, and they may take a transverse or a longitudinal form.

The great ergs are probably the most spectacular of all desert landscapes. These fixed, prehistoric forms can reach up to 400 m in height. There has always been much speculation as to how they came into being. One theory was that flying sand formed mounds when two great wind systems met head-on. The long straight ridges were seen as the remains of troughs caused by erosion in the gaps between the mounds. The most recent research, however, has come to the conclusion that the only model which can show the origins of the draas and all their attendant phenomena is the double helix. This complex current-based model explains why the spaces between the draas are equal over many kilometres, why ergs finish when the ground becomes uneven, and why there can never be such a thing as a small erg. The causes are connected with permanently high wind velocity, which existed during the ice ages as a result of massive differences in temperature on a scale that can no longer be found. This also explains why draas are no longer formed today. The idea that seas of dunes are constantly in motion just like the oceans is therefore as false as the belief that deserts were once seabeds.

'If one stays on the crest itself, where the sand is a firm, compressed mass, it's easier to move. Although we all tried to keep warm by walking, we were almost paralysed with cold in the strong southwest wind, which never stopped for a second. The sand swirled from the crests of the dunes just like ostrich feathers, and everything disappeared in yellowish grey mist. One can see how the sharp contours of the crests change position under the impact of the wind.'

Sven Hedin

# CHANGES IN THE SAHARAN CLIMATE AND LANDSCAPE

PROFESSOR DR KLAUS GIESSNER

Thanks to the many finds that have been made in the Sahara, scientific research over the last forty years has been able to put together a model of the changes which have taken place in the climate and the landscape. There are still gaps in the picture, and some details remain speculative, but the main arguments are now well documented. We know, for instance, that most of the relief was formed in prehistoric times, when the climate was not arid, and the decisive onset of aridity occurred between 3.1 and 2.6 million years ago. Since then, the degree of aridity and the borders between the moister peripheral zones and the upland regions (Hoggar, Tibesti, Aïr) have shifted during Saharan history, although the basic climate has not changed.

TRIASSIC TO CRETACEOUS: 251 TO 65 MILLION YEARS AGO   During the Triassic period (251–208 million years ago), the unified land masses of the old southern continent of Gondwanaland (Africa, South America, Antarctica and Australia) created a distinct continentality and aridity. During the Jurassic period (208–144 million years ago), this great block began to break up, and the southern continents started to assume the shape they have today. In the Cretaceous period (144–65 million years ago), plate tectonics continued this development, with South America and Antarctica drifting away from Africa. In the early Tertiary (65 million years ago), the situation and configuration of the continents were virtually as they are now, but Africa drifted a further 15° to the north.

THE MIDDLE TERTIARY: EOCENE – OLIGOCENE, 65 TO 23.8 MILLION YEARS AGO
During the Eocene and Oligocene epochs, the climate was humid-tropical to alternating humid, which led to intensive weathering and bleaching of the crystalline basement rocks.

Five thousand years ago, the Sahara was considerably moister and greener than it is today. Rock pictures from former times depict elephants, rhinos and giraffes, as well as creatures from the savanna. This often gives rise to the false premise that the desert is only a few thousand years old. In reality, it goes back more than two million years, but the aridity was frequently broken by periods of relative moisture, the so-called pluvial stages.

Rock paintings in Ennedi, Chad.

# Life and survival in the desert
## DESERT PLANTS

In deserts the variety of plants and animals is drastically reduced. In the Sahara itself there are only 1,400 known sorts of plant – a number which in the tropical rain forests would be contained within just a few square kilometres. The shortage or absence of vegetation is a characteristic of deserts, and with climatic criteria, the presence or disappearance of particular plants is a reliable indicator of their boundaries. The northern edge of the Sahara is marked by the presence of alfa grass, and the southern edge by cram-cram grass.

Lack of water and the extreme temperatures are the main enemies of plant life in deserts. They impose rigid limits on life in general and vegetation in particular. Plants, unlike animals, cannot seek out water or shade, or migrate to wetter regions; they are compelled to adapt to the conditions of their environment and to develop appropriate strategies of survival. We shall begin with a general survey, and then examine three typical examples of such strategies.

Lack of water and high ground, and air temperatures are a constant threat and, even if plants may be more resistant to these conditions than animals, a temperature of over 50°C will coagulate the protoplasm. The high saline content of many desert soils limits the growth of plants, although some – like halophytes – have adapted themselves. In the Sahara and the Lut there is no visible vegetation over hundreds of thousands of square kilometres. Yet, they still contain traces of life. Near the Algerian border town of In Guezzam, soil samples have shown that a single gramme of earth contained 10,000 bacteria and 3,300 fungi.

At first sight, it might appear that the plant life of the world's deserts differs widely from one to another, but there are in fact many common features. This could point to a common origin – perhaps from a time when the continents were bound together – but it could also derive from the fact that under the selective pressures imposed by similar conditions, plants develop similar forms and strategies. The term used for both flora and fauna is convergence.

In the Iranian Lut and in parts of the Sahara, hundreds of thousands of square kilometres appear to be without any form of vegetation. However, traces of life are still to be found there. Soil tests have shown that a gramme of earth may contain up to 10,000 bacteria and 3,300 fungal spores. In many deserts, a single gramme of earth may contain up to 10 million micro-organisms.

Joshua tree in the Mojave, USA.

# DESERT WILDLIFE

Deserts pose a massive challenge to animals. Life is a constant struggle for survival in a hostile environment, where they must protect themselves against overheating, endure extreme variations in temperature, make do with what little there is in the way of food, put up with high doses of ultra-violet radiation, and battle against the wind, which can dehydrate them and transport smaller creatures to even more hostile surroundings. Predators find little shelter, and their prey little protection. Furthermore, there is a permanent shortage of water, and evaporation continually causes them to lose what they have. At least two-thirds of their bodies consist of water, and if this proportion drops, they can no longer function. Because of all these factors, the variety of species is extremely limited compared to other habitats. In the Sahara, for instance, there are only fifty species of mammals, most of them rodents. Darkling beetles, on the other hand, have adapted remarkably well, and there are no less than 340 varieties.

To detail every type of desert animal would expand this volume to bursting point, and so I shall just give a brief survey of the fauna, and then describe the strategies that enable them to survive. The camel, however, as the desert animal par excellence, will have a chapter to itself.

## INVERTEBRATES

Aridity is a powerful agent of selection among the invertebrates, because for many of them – snails and isopods, for instance – the need for water is incompatible with the desert climate. Arachnids, however, are often perfectly adapted to such conditions. The best known and the most feared of these, on account of its venomous sting, is the scorpion – a primeval creature whose form and structure has barely altered in 400 million years. There are many other kinds of arachnid to be found in the desert, including wind scorpions, pseudoscorpions, spiders,

'I consider it impossible on a day's trek through the Sahara, even in the dead regions of the Erg Chech, even in the Tanezrouft, not to find some sign of animal life – quite apart from the flies that swarm round people. One will at the very least find the tracks of a beetle, an ant, a feather, or the remains of a locust. But one has to look closely, with the eyes of a naturalist.'

Théodore Monod

A giraffe at the Ol Doinyo Lengai in the Rift Valley.

# THE CAMEL AND THE DESERT

DR ULRICH WERNERY

Over a long period of time, the camel has developed an extraordinary range of physiological and morphological adaptations to the extremes of its environment, and for those who live in the desert it is the most important of all domesticated animals. The camel produces not only milk, wool and meat, but it also facilitates trade over thousands of kilometres, and its resistance to fatal animal diseases makes it indispensable to all the desert peoples. It is scarcely surprising that the Bedouins call it 'Ata Allah' (Gift of God).

One of the most striking physical features of the camelid family is the structure of their feet. They do not have hooves but move on two toes, which are united at the sole by a web of leathery skin that consists of fat and elastic tissue. This anatomical peculiarity gives padded protection, prevents the animal from sinking too deep, and keeps the heat of the sand off its legs. Camelids always give the impression of stepping high because they do not have any real fold in the knee. The kneecap is visible beneath the skin, but the thigh is not joined in its entire length to the rump. The gait is generally ambling, with front and hind legs moving evenly forward and back – a movement that uses up a minimum of energy.

The oldest fossil find goes back to the early Tertiary in North America, between 60 and 50 million years ago. At that time, the camelids were the size of a hare, and they branched out into eight families. Five million years ago, there were two main branches: the camelina and the lamina, and it was at this time that the camelina crossed the land bridge which is now the Bering Strait and entered northern Asia. It was from these that the Old World camels descended. They spread further west, and during the Pleistocene epoch even reached as far as Europe, North and East Africa and eastern Asia. Both the dromedary (*Camelus dromedarius*) and the Bactrian camel (*Camelus bactrianus*) existed by then. When these Old World camels

'For travelling through the Sahara, the meheri is man's indispensable companion, and indeed a journey across the great desert would be an impossibility without this animal. It carries large loads – and has an extraordinary sense of direction. It is not uncommon for caravans that have lost their way to be led to an oasis or a well simply by their camels' instincts, for when they have had nothing to drink for some time, they are able to scent water from a great distance.'

Gerhard Rohlfs

migrated northeast, the lamina went south over the Panamanian land bridge and settled in the South American countries. Today they are known as New World camels, humpless camels, or South American camelids. There are four distinct species: the llama (*Lama glama*) and the alpaca (*Lama pacos*), both of which are tame, and the guanaco (*Lama guanaco*) and the vicuña (*Lama vicugna*), which are both wild.

In North America camels became extinct 10,000 years ago, probably because of intensive hunting by Native Americans. In South America, however, there are between seven and eight million New World camels. Llamas and alpacas have been domesticated for the last 7,000 years, which is a unique achievement.

All camelids have the same number of chromosomes. They are phylogenetically related, and so they can be cross-bred. Common hybridizations are between bactrian (m) and dromedary (f) – known as a tulu – between dromedary (m) and guanaco (f), and between dromedary (m) and llama (f).

DNA analyses have shown that the llama is the domesticated form of the wild guanaco, and the alpaca the domesticated form of the wild vicuña. The latter lives in the Altiplano (3,700–5,000 m high). It is protected against the icy cold by its thick coat, whose value as a natural textile has preserved it from extinction. Because of the extremely thin air, the vicuña's heart has become greatly enlarged in the course of evolution, and its relative weight is more than fifty per cent greater than that of similar-sized mammals. In addition, the oval red blood cells of New World camelids are richly oxygenated, which again is an extremely important adaptation for life at a high altitude. Even in the thin atmosphere of the Andes, at 4,500 m above sea level, the haemoglobin is able to process the oxygen efficiently in the lungs and to transport it to the rest of the body.

Recent osteological examinations of dromedary and Bactrian skeletons have shown that there were actually two different kinds of Old World camel and not, as had previously been believed, a single species. Although the wild ancestry of the Bactrian seems to have been confirmed by prehistoric cave paintings in Kazakhstan and Mongolia, the dromedary probably evolved from the Thomas giant camel (*Camelus thomasi*, named after a French palaeontolo-

Alpaca in Bolivia.

gist), which lived in North Africa and the Negev desert during the last Ice Age, and then became extinct.

Today there are some 20 million Old World camels in existence, of which two million are Bactrians. All dromedaries are domesticated. In the Gobi desert and in China's most westerly province, Sinkiang, there are 600–800 wild Bactrians, but they are threatened with extinction. These camels are smaller and thinner than the domesticated ones, have two small, pointed humps, and live exclusively on salt water. In Sinkiang they have been a protected species for several years, living in the Arjin Shan Lop Nur Nature Reserve, which is about the size of Poland. Old World camels used to be exported. One hundred years ago, dromedaries were taken to Australia and used as working animals or beasts of burden. They were also sent to southern Africa (Namibia), Europe and North America.

Camels are at home in the treeless arid zones. Their staple food is the hard, dry flora of the steppes. Apart from grass, which is available in small quantities only during the wetter season, they eat rushes, bark, herbs and spiny plants such as acacia. Camels do not indulge in defoliation, and they preserve their environment. They are out-and-out browsers that make the most of every mouthful, and with their long eyelashes and hairs around the mouth, they also help to pollinate bushes, grass and trees.

The many uses that human beings have found for camelids have resulted in different races. The Arabs distinguish between some twenty races of dromedary, which vary considerably in value and usefulness. The short, plump and bulky types, for instance, are the beasts of burden; the lighter, thinner, taller and elegant form is perfect for riding, and is the only variety that can manage the huge desert crossings. A particularly swift and nimble type is the mehari, a thoroughbred dromedary comparable to the finest of racehorses and capable of covering 110–120 km a day with no effort at all. The nomads sing the praises of the Sudanese bisharin for its fleetness of foot and its thirst resistance, while the speed of racing camels is worth millions of dollars to their owners on the Arabian peninsula.

There are many misapprehensions concerning the camel's water system: many people believe that the humps and stomach are secret reservoirs. It is, however, far more accurate to

The dromedary was first introduced into Australia in 1840. It was much more suitable than horses for exploring and opening up the vast arid regions. With the arrival of lorries, however, the dromedaries were let loose in the wilderness of the outback, where to the annoyance of the livestock farmers they proceeded to thrive and multiply. There are an estimated 100,000 dromedaries in Australia today.

Wild camels in the Gobi.

Camel in Mauritania.

say that camels cannot store water as such, but like no other creature on Earth they are blessed with effective mechanisms for retaining their fluids instead of losing them through perspiration, excrement and urine. The humps store energy for when it is needed, and they consist mainly of fat which provides emergency rations when there is a food shortage.

In the rainy season, camels can take in all the fluids they need from the green plants that they eat, and they can survive for months without fresh water. They can cope with long periods of thirst, and can do without any water at all for up to three weeks. They can lose up to forty per cent of their water without suffering any damage, and once they do drink, they make up for the loss in an amazingly short time. It has been noted that camels can take in 200 litres of water in just fifteen minutes. In any other mammal, this would result in a form of intoxication in which the red blood corpuscles would burst, leading to certain death. The camel, however, has a unique ability to absorb huge quantities of fluids very quickly, and thus fill the parched body cells. The crucial factor here is the compartment (the equivalent of the rumen – the three chambers of a camel's stomach are called compartments). This can hold huge quantities of liquid before it goes into the intestines.

When most mammals – including humans – sweat, much of the water is taken from the blood, or to be more precise from the plasma, which therefore becomes thicker; when the camel sweats, however, the water is taken mainly from the alimentary canal. This keeps the blood thin so that circulation is not affected. In order to minimize the loss of fluids through perspiration, dehydrated camels can regulate the temperature of their blood according to the temperature outside. To keep the body stabilized at 37°C, nearly all mammals – again including humans – use the cooling mechanism that operates through sweat evaporation. In a dehydrated camel, however, this mechanism only begins to work at a temperature of 40–42°C, which saves both fluids and energy. Furthermore, the camel's temperature can sink to 34°C, thus getting rid of warmth during the relative coolness of the night in order to lay in a cold store for the heat of the following day – again a mode of energy saving.

High body temperatures over any length of time would have dangerous consequences even for the camel, with the brain cells and the retina particularly vulnerable, but once again nature has endowed it with special protection: with its long nose it has an extraordinary, inbuilt cooling mechanism. Tests carried out in Kenya by the Norwegian physiologist Knut Schmidt-Nielsen showed that camels breathe in the hot desert air which dries up the mucous membrane of the nose. Large areas of the nasal lining therefore become hygroscopic (i.e. capable of absorbing moisture), and so when the camel breathes out, the steam-filled air from the lungs passes over these dry surfaces, which then absorb the moisture; normally air that is breathed out is full of steam, but with the camel it comes out dry. The moisture absorbed within the nose goes on to cool the carotid rete, a network of vessels close to the long turbinate bones. The blood cooled within this network reduces the temperature of the blood in the parallel jugular vein, which carries blood from the nose to the heart. As this venous blood flows to the heart, it cools the hot arterial blood that is on its way from the heart to supply the heat-sensitive brain and eye cells. This simple but unique counter-current protects the endangered cells from overheating. The camel's brain and eyes are kept 4–6°C cooler than the rest of its body.

Another of the camel's special talents is to conserve fluids when it defecates. Cows lose 20–40 litres of fluid a day in their excrement, whereas camels lose only 1.3 litres. They excrete tiny, dry pellets because they have special cells in their rectum which extract the fluid from the stools. The structure and function of their kidneys also help in the conservation of water. The loop of Henle is four to six times longer than that of a cow, which concentrates the urine and also slows its flow. The structure of the kidneys also enables camels to drink seawater and to eat salty plants, and this has helped the wild Bactrians of China to survive.

The camel supplies meat, milk, wool and dung, the latter of which is used as fuel. All of these make it a significant economic factor in developing countries. In Somalia and Sudan, millions of nomads live on camel milk, which is immensely rich in nutrients and is often the most important source of Vitamin C in the human diet. The Vitamin C content is four to six times greater than that of cow's milk, and the yield is some 10–20 litres a day. The camel is unquestionably indispensable for the inhabitants of the desert, whose survival has since time immemorial depended on the ability of this 'ship of the desert' to adapt itself to the harsh conditions of desert life.

Salt caravan in the Ténéré.

# DESERT PEOPLE

Living conditions in the desert create massive problems for those who live there. There are a number of factors and characteristics that all contribute to making the desert an extremely hostile environment, including a shortage of food and drinking water, extremes of temperature and aridity, exposure to the sun, a lack of roads, the sheer expanse, isolation and inaccessibility, especially in cases of emergency.

Unlike plants and animals, human beings are not physically or morphologically adapted to extreme conditions, apart from the darker pigmentation of the skin that is common to most desert-dwellers. Nevertheless, behavioural adaptations and technical aids help humans both to live in and to cross the desert. In the heat of the day, they can withdraw to their homes, they can dig wells to tap the groundwater, they can travel by camel or by truck over hundreds of kilometres, using maps or satellite technology or simply a refined sense of direction, and they can dress in clothes that will protect them against radiation and dehydration.

Being warm-blooded mammals, human beings must keep their temperature between 36.5° and 37.5°C. They can survive between 33°C and 42°C, but beyond these limits the cells cease to function normally, the metabolism breaks down, and the inevitable result is death. A naked man would be unlikely to survive a single summer's evening in the central Sahara without shade and water.

There are three ways of life that have enabled humans to inhabit the desert over thousands of years: oasis dwelling, hunting and gathering, and nomadism. We now know that the old picture of hunters and gatherers becoming nomads and then later settling down as farmers is inaccurate. Even though the first humans were undoubtedly hunters and gatherers, a few thousand years ago all three ways of life existed concurrently.

Skin colour is a form of human adaptation to the environment. According to recent genetic research, it goes back in evolutionary history to the hunters and gatherers. The stronger the sun, and the more intense the ultraviolet radiation, the more the skin will be darkened by its melanin. It is this dark pigment that prevents the dangerous ultraviolet radiation from penetrating into the body.

Sandstorm in Mauritania.

River oasis in the High Atlas Mountains, Morocco.

'The Ghat oasis, stretching from west to east with its dum-palm and talha trees, offers a very welcome refuge to the weary desert traveller. For me, on my first journey so far to the south, the sight of the dum-palm was a relief that brought much pleasure to the eye.'

Gerhard Rohlfs

OASES   In the desert, an oasis is an enclave – a small island of life in the vast and hostile ocean of sand. It is also, however, a link with the outside world. Oases are always found near springs, groundwater or rivers. They may be uninhabited or intensively farmed, in which case they are often extended by irrigation. They are not only outposts for trade and traffic, but they often look back over a long and complex history. Oases such as Chinguetti in Mauritania or Kashgar on the Silk Road became centres of religion, science, art and literature. The same is true of river oases. The pharaonic culture in the Nile Valley, and the cultural centres on the Euphrates and the Tigris are well-known examples.

Most oases are in the Old World arid belt, but there are also some in the New World, such as the river oases in Peru. The main crop in the Old World arid belt is the date palm, although there is a wide range of other cultivated vegetation. In many Central Asian oases, winter temperatures are too low for the date palm, and so there are poplar, peach, apricot and fig trees instead. The almost mythical vision of oases that one finds in novels and films goes back to the accounts of European explorers, who after the ordeal of crossing the desert would experience an oasis as a kind of seventh heaven. In devastating contrast to this vision is the destruction of oases in Arabia and the Sahara because of the oil boom, and in Central Asia because of the political ends pursued by the former Soviet Union and by China. Structures and traditions that had lasted for hundreds of years have been destroyed for ever, palm groves have been left to wither, and whole villages have been abandoned.

Almost as a kind of by-product, the oil boom has created new settlements which are called high-tech oases. In the search for oil, great reserves of groundwater have been found, sometimes as far down as 2,000 m, and so massive pumps bring it to the surface, where sprinklers and other devices water great fields of grain and alfalfa in the middle of the desert. Often the yield bears no relation to the financial cost, but a major economic success has been the river oases on the Peruvian coast, which produce large quantities of fruit for export.

HUNTERS AND GATHERERS   The first human beings to settle in the warm, dry regions of the Earth were hunter-gatherers. These regions, where primates stood and moved about on their hind legs in order to get a better view, were not deserts but steppes or semi-deserts. Even a few centuries ago, the hunter-gatherer culture would not have been found either in the hot deserts, where they would have been driven out by the increasing aridity, or in the cold deserts of Central Asia, which they probably never inhabited anyway. The last hunter-gatherer cultures were probably those of the Aboriginal Australians, the Bushmen of the Kalahari, and the Native Americans in the deserts of North America. The rich flora and fauna gave them ample resources for thousands of years. The older generation of Bushmen can still identify one hundred edible plants in the Kalahari, and they used to collect plants for food and drink, medicine and building. Great herds of gazelles and antelopes once provided the hunters with all the meat they needed. The lives of these hunter-gatherers were naturally migratory, for as soon as resources diminished, and there were no more plants or animals in an area, they would simply move on. They never had many possessions: sticks for digging or throwing, skins, and containers made from the bark of trees, all of which could be transported on foot.

To a greater degree even than the nomads and peasant farmers, hunter-gatherers were pushed out by the advance of so-called civilization. The traditional way of life of the Aboriginal Australians, the Bushmen and the Native Americans has disappeared for ever. The few groups that survived this sometimes systematic extermination were nevertheless robbed of their livelihood by the restriction or destruction of their hunting-grounds, and whole cultures were thereby destroyed before we could benefit from their knowledge and their ideas.

NOMADS  In the evolution of human culture, nomadism should not be regarded as a primitive stage of transition. It is, rather, a way of life that is uniquely suited to the vast, barren expanses of the Old World arid belt. With a few exceptions, the classic pastoral nomadism is confined to this belt, which extends from Mauritania in the west to China. In Australia the animals were not suitable, and in North America no real effort was made to breed the llamas that would have been ideal.

Nomad culture is multifaceted. There are full nomads and semi-nomads, the former living exclusively on their cattle, while the latter also pursue other activities such as farming, trade and transport. Transhumance is not regarded as a form of nomadism because the families do not own the herds; they live in fixed abodes and move between summer and winter pastures.

Kanuri children collecting wood near Fachi.

Nomadism can be classified according to the kind of animals that are kept: depending on the conditions set by the environment, these may be camels, dromedaries, horses, cows, yaks, sheep or goats. There are also distinctions to be made between the types of migration – vertical or horizontal, near or far, episodic or periodic, planned or unplanned – and the forms of accommodation: tents, yurts, screens, caves.

The animals vary from one region to another. In Mongolia the speciality is horses, in the Tibetan highlands yaks, in Central Asia camels, between Rajasthan and Mauritania dromedaries, and in the Sahel and East Africa cattle. They all have the same system of evaluation: the number and the outward appearance of the animals will determine the fortune of the owner and his standing in the world. In former times, animals would only be slaughtered for personal use or for special occasions, and market-orientated breeding was an alien concept. Today the economic situation is such that many nomads regularly sell their cattle to dealers.

Nomadism has played an important part in human history. The Scythians, Parthians, Bedouins, Huns and Mongols all established and destroyed empires, and waged war on the settlers or lived in symbiosis with them. The depressing situation of today is the result of many different developments. Firstly, political conditions changed with the European colonization of Africa, Arabia and Asia, while in the USSR and China economic and political agendas resulted in more and more restrictions on the nomads. In Africa, the arbitrary national boundaries drawn by the colonial powers when they divided the continent up again curtailed freedom of movement, as well as leading to military conflicts which the nomadic peoples could never win. Within the Soviet sphere of influence, the policy of collective farming put an end to the nomads' way of life, and their living space was drastically reduced by their traditional grazing grounds being turned into farms, military zones and national parks. Roads and modern forms of transport took away the economic basis of the caravans, and opened up the regions to external market forces. In addition to all this, overexploitation of the natural resources led to ecological disaster in the form of desertification.

What is the position of the nomads today in the various countries of the Old World arid belt? The situation of the Reguibat in the Sahara is dramatic. As a result of the conflict in the western

Himba nomads milking a cow.

Tubu tent scaffolding, Chad.

Sahara, these people have been living for decades in camps, waiting in vain to return to their meagre pastures. The mobility of the Tuaregs is limited by the fact that their traditional grounds have been divided up between Algeria, Libya, Mali and Niger, and moving their herds means not only crossing national borders, but also coming into conflict with local farmers. Droughts have driven many Tuaregs into city slums and temporary camps, and a Tuareg uprising in Niger and Mali that lasted from 1991 till 1995 cost many lives. On the Arabian peninsula, it was the oil boom that put an end to the Bedouins' traditional way of life. Instead of the herds going out to pasture, their fodder and water is brought to them by the truckload, they are watched over by foreign workers, and their owners keep them merely as a pastime. In Iran and Afghanistan, nomadism has survived in spite of severe political pressures. The economic situation of the Afghan nomads is, however, extremely precarious. Nomadism in Czarist Russia had already been under threat from colonization, and the final nail was driven in by socialist collectivization under Stalin. Nomads were forced to enter work teams and to become employees of the State, while the herds themselves belonged to the *kolkhoz* (collective farms). After the break-up of the Soviet Union, there has been a limited return to nomadic values, and a similar development has occurred in Mongolia. There it has actually been more successful than in Central Asia, as awareness of ecological factors in the pasture lands survived the period of Socialist rule, and reprivatization of cattle farming has made this the most important industry in the country. In China, the Han people took over the nomad regions from the 1950s onwards, forcing the nomads themselves either to work in the communes or to withdraw to the most remote areas. The liberalization of agriculture towards the end of the 1970s brought about an improvement in their living conditions, and they were given cattle and pasture land as the Chinese authorities recognized that this land would otherwise be left fallow. It remains to be seen, however, what effects China's headlong rush to modernization will have on its nomads.

Does nomadism have a future? The above account inevitably raises doubts. However, FAO (Food and Agriculture Organization) statistics show that potential grazing land covers an area of no less than 3.5 billion hectares. In view of the population explosion, neither individual countries nor humankind in general can afford to let these vast tracts of land go unused through the

Well in Mali.

Tuaregs in Mali.

disappearance of the nomads. On the other hand, regional overexploitation must also be avoided, since the consequences can be dire. Officials in the various states concerned, and the misguided policies of development aid organizations, have in the last fifty years done everything possible to persuade the nomads to settle, but the economic, ecological and psychological effects of such policies have been appalling – to which the slums in Nouakchott, Teheran and Urumchi bear testament. The nomads themselves are scarcely ever consulted on the question of how they would like to live. Governments and development aid organizations should give them all the support they need, because nomadism remains the only ecologically suitable way to use the grazing areas of the world's deserts and semi-deserts.

DESERTIFICATION   Desertification has become an international catchword, but it is often misused to describe a climatically induced expansion of desert regions. Horst Mensching, a well-known expert on the subject, defines desertification as: 'Processes in arid regions and their often densely populated peripheral zones which through human impact have led to ecological degradation and the destruction of natural resources.' Droughts play an important part in anthropogenic degradation and show up the consequences with devastating clarity, but they are not the cause.

Decisive factors in the process of desertification are tree-felling, the expansion of farming into regions of sparse rainfall, and overexploitation of natural pastures. The pressures of population growth exacerbate the problem. The consequences affect innumerable facets of the ecosystem, including the condition of the soil and the water supply in relation to drainage and infiltration. Crusts form on the surface of the earth, and these increase surface drainage, leading in turn to more erosion. The finer components of the soil are washed away, the fertility of the soil is reduced, and consequently more areas become barren. The earth is increasingly exposed to the vagaries of the wind, and the disappearance of vegetation increases evaporation, so that less rain gets through to the ground, which gradually becomes arid. The result of all this is a man-made desert.

These processes take place in an insular fashion – around wells or villages, for example – but they can link up and lead to the degradation of large stretches of land. It is difficult to quantify the effects, but in the Sahel region alone during the last fifty years some 650,000 km$^2$ have turned into desert or at best have become infertile and incapable of regeneration. Worldwide, the yearly loss of agricultural land is estimated at 50,000–60,000 km$^2$, much of it in Africa because over half of this continent is arid. Over a billion people all over the world are believed to have been affected by the consequences of desertification. The social consequences alone are enormous: the destruction of natural resources makes it impossible for farmers as well as nomads to earn a living, and individuals and whole families migrate to the cities, which creates new sets of problems. Gradually governments and development aid organizations are waking up to the explosive nature of this situation, and are bringing in measures, ranging from the introduction of new farming techniques to a ban on tree-felling.

Relatively simple techniques taken over from traditional forms of agriculture can limit erosion and prevent desertification. Small dams erected parallel to a slope can stop the soil from being worn away. Where the land is flat, mounds and dams of vegetation will prevent the rainwater from escaping.

# Exploring the Deserts
# THE HISTORY OF DESERT EXPLORATION

Anyone looking at high resolution satellite pictures or logging onto the countless websites will find it difficult to imagine how little our forefathers knew about the geography of the Earth. As recently as the nineteenth century, the interior of Africa and Australia was a blank on the map. The history of desert exploration is, of course, part of the history of exploration generally, but deserts were never an end in themselves: Marco Polo, for instance, crossed many deserts, but his goal was the court of the great khans in China. Nevertheless, his notes contained valuable information about the deserts of Asia.

The starting point of these voyages of discovery was Europe. Only in the West was there the requisite blend of curiosity to penetrate new territories and an aggressive desire to trade, which itself combined missionary zeal with military conquest in the endless search for raw materials, markets and luxury goods. It is true that Ibn Battutah was a famous Arabian explorer, and Abu Bakari II, the ruler of Mali, sent shipping expeditions across the Atlantic, but for the most part the great cultures of Japan, China and Africa, not to mention the Aztecs and the Maya, evidently felt little desire to go forth and see the world.

Social conditions dictated that – until well into the nineteenth century – exploration was the province almost exclusively of men, although Alexandra David-Néel and Isabelle Eberhardt were notable exceptions. The explorers included scholars, adventurers, merchants, missionaries and soldiers. They were often on official business. Convinced of the superiority of their own civilization, they rarely had any respect for the natives. Men such as Heinrich Barth were very much the exception. His principal interest was to advance the cause of scientific knowledge.

By the beginning of the twentieth century, ninety-five per cent of the Earth had been explored, and the few remaining unexplored regions included the deserts of Central Asia and Arabia.

Alexandra David-Néel (1868–1969) crossed the Gobi desert in 1923, to enter the 'Forbidden City' of Lhasa in Tibet. She travelled through regions that no European had ever seen, and gathered detailed information about the people and the geography. Isabelle Eberhardt (1877–1904) disguised herself as an Arab and travelled through the sands of the northern Sahara.

Original map by Heinrich Barth.

In 1298, Marco Polo was taken prisoner by the Genoese. He recounted his adventures to a fellow captive named Rustichello, a writer from Pisa, who wrote them down. This travel book soon became famous under the title of *The Book of Wonders*. At first, people were sceptical as to its authenticity, but later the content was confirmed by other travellers.

Long before the great explorers crossed the deserts, we may assume that others had also made the journey, but we shall never know for sure whether merchants from Carthage, military patrols, Roman deserters, pilgrims or adventurers did penetrate the mysteries of the Sahara before the advent of René Caillié and Heinrich Barth. The history of exploration is also the history of the natives who accompanied the explorers, and without whose expert knowledge even Sven Hedin could never have succeeded in crossing the deserts of Central Asia. Generation after generation of these native guides had been familiar with all the landscapes, mountains and routes which the explorers then claimed to have discovered for themselves, but their reports rarely mention the part played by their guides.

THE DISCOVERY OF THE ASIAN DESERTS   This began with a military campaign. In 330 BC, Alexander the Great (356–323 BC) marched his army over the Hindu Kush into the north of Afghanistan, then across the Syr-Dayra into Punjab. There, however, a mutiny compelled him to turn back, and he proceeded to cross the deserts of Baluchistan while his commander-in-chief, Craterus, tried to cross the Lut with his elephants. The Roman Empire traded with Asia by way of the Silk Road, and mounted military campaigns against Arabia, all of which helped to increase knowledge of the Asian and Arabian deserts.

MARCO POLO   In the Middle Ages it was above all Marco Polo (1254–1324) who, through his journey to China, made Europe aware of the great deserts of Asia. He was the son of a Venetian merchant, and in 1271 he accompanied his father and uncle to China. They travelled through Persia to the ancient caravan city of Balkh, crossed the mountain passes of the Pamir, and continued along the Silk Road. They then crossed the desert at Lop Nor, and in 1275 arrived in Kambalu (now Beijing). Marco Polo remained in China until 1292, and became a confidant of the great Kublai Khan, who used him as an envoy and even made him governor of Yang Chow in southern China. In 1292, however, the Venetians left China and travelled by sea and land back to Venice, arriving in 1295.

IBN BATTUTAH   The history of the journeys made by Ibn Battutah (1304–68) remained unknown in Europe for almost 500 years, even though he was the only traveller who could stand comparison with Marco Polo. He dictated his reports to a scholar named Ibn Dschuzaj, and they constitute a remarkable record of both a Christian and a Muslim world view at the end of the Middle Ages. He was born in Tangiers, and at the age of twenty went on a pilgrimage to Mecca. He did not return to his Moroccan homeland until twenty-four years later. He was a cadi (a minor Muslim judge), and practised this profession whenever he journeyed to Islamic countries. From Mecca he made many journeys – to Mesopotamia and Persia, Yemen and East Africa, the Vogla, through Afghanistan to China, and even to Timbuktu. In total he covered 120,000 km – three times as much as Marco Polo.

In the nineteenth century, the geographer Ferdinand Freiherr von Richthofen (1833–1905) and the Russian general Nikolay Mikhaylovich Przhevalsky (or Przewalski) (1839–88) both undertook journeys that yielded new information about the deserts of Asia. Between 1868 and 1872, Richthofen made seven expeditions to China, and his pioneering work made him the father of modern geography. At almost the same time, Przhevalsky crossed the Gobi desert, reached the Qaidam Basin, crossed the Ordos desert, and entered northern Mongolia. In 1876–77, he passed through the Takla Makan on his way to the Tarim Basin, and in 1879–80 he finally reached Tibet. In the steppes of Asia, Przhevalsky came upon a hitherto unknown type of wild horse, which was named Przewalski's horse after him.

SVEN HEDIN    Sven Hedin (1865–1952) became world famous for his exploration of uncharted regions of Asia. After staying in Persia as an interpreter for a diplomatic mission, he remained in Tehran and from there set out on his first expedition to Central Asia through Merv, Buchara and Samarkand to Kashgar and Lake Issyk-Kul. Further expeditions followed. Hedin was particularly interested in the movement of waters (e.g. the 'wandering lake' of Lop Nor) and in Tibet. His popular scientific books ran into many editions and were translated into thirty languages. Today there is a more critical view of him, largely because he was in close contact with the Nazis and remained an admirer of Hitler even after the Second World War.

The deserts of Iran and Central Asia were explored by Russians: Buhse crossed the Great Kavir in 1849, and Khanikov the central Lut in 1858. Meanwhile, the deserts of Arabia were blank areas on the map for a very long time. Not until 1931 did the British explorer Bertram

Sven Hedin

353

Thomas (1892–1950) cross the Rub al-Khali, 'The Empty Quarter', though he took an easy route. In 1932, he was followed by his compatriot Harry St John Philby (1885–1960), who crossed the western part on a journey of 3,000 km. It was only in 1946 and 1948, however, that a complete crossing was achieved, this time by the Englishman Wilfred Thesiger (1910–2003), the last of the great eccentric British explorers.

THE DISCOVERY OF THE AUSTRALIAN DESERTS  It took a long time for the interior of Australia to be opened up. After this – the fifth continent – had been discovered in around 1600, it remained virtually ignored because it seemed to offer no commercial prospects. By the beginning of the nineteenth century, only the coastal regions had been explored and partly settled in by whites. Owing to insuperable transport problems, Europeans were for a long time very hesitant to set foot in the interior – there were no beasts of burden, no oases or tracks, and not even any guides. While Europe was all agog at the expeditions of Heinrich Barth, Livingstone and Stanley, few adventurous or scholarly souls dared to wander into the Australian unknown.

In 1839–40, Edward John Eyre (1815–1901) explored the lower reaches of the Murray and the Flinders Range, and he came upon various lakes, including Torrens, Eyre, Gregory and Blanche. In 1840–41, he went from Fowler Bay near Adelaide to the King George Sound on the western coast. Virtually single-handed he thus managed to cross the desert regions of South Australia, and his reports, which contain detailed information about the Aboriginal Australians, are today regarded as major works of Australian literature. Charles Sturt (1795–1869) made three expeditions between 1827 and 1845, and reached almost as far as latitude 24° south – though even this did not mean that he had crossed the entire continent.

LUDWIG LEICHHARDT  The German explorer Ludwig Leichhardt (1813–48) attempted this feat in 1846, when he set out from Sydney with the intention of crossing central Australia overland. His destination was Perth, but he never got there. Expeditions were sent to search for him, but although they came back with new geographical information, his fate remained unknown. One such expedition was led by John Forrest (1847–1918), and in 1870 he succeeded in crossing western Australia from Perth to Adelaide. The Scotsman John McDouall

Ludwig Leichhardt has been virtually forgotten in Germany, but his name is still famous in Australia. In 1844–45, he became the first European to cross the continent from east to north. He was born in the Niederlausitz, studied in Berlin and Göttingen, and emigrated to Australia in 1841. On his legendary expeditions, he collected many unknown plants, some of which are still reserved in Sydney. Thirty-three plants, including a eucalyptus and a palm, have been named after him, and there is even a district in Sydney that bears his name.

Stuart (1815–66) had taken part in Sturt's expedition of 1844, and fourteen years later he crossed the continent from north to south, with the aid of sixty-nine horses. The highway that today runs from Darwin to Port Augusta via Alice Springs bears his name.

In 1872, Peter Egerton Warburton (1813–89) set out from Adelaide with the aim of reaching Perth via Alice Springs. With camels as his beasts of burden, he crossed the Great Victoria Desert to the western Australian frontier, but was then forced by lack of water to turn north-west in the direction of known settlements. From 1870 onwards, exploration of the central Australian deserts was made infinitely easier by telegraph lines.

ERNEST GILES   The explorer Ernest Giles (1835–97) undertook several expeditions into the interior of Australia. In 1875, he explored the regions along the east-west route. Together with his camels, he started out from Port Augusta, crossed the Great Victoria Desert, and 4,000 km later arrived in Perth. In 1880, he was awarded the Gold Medal by the Royal Geographical Society, but he did not receive a penny for his pains. The last great explorer of Australia was forced to work for meagre pay as a guard at a goldfield, and he died in abject poverty.

Nasca lines in Peru.

THE DISCOVERY OF THE AMERICAN DESERTS   Exploration of North America started on the East Coast. It began in the seventeenth century, but it was not the aim to find deserts. They became the target of monks who set out from the Mexican highlands. One of them, the Jesuit Eusebio Kino (1645–1711) from south Tirol, covered almost 35,000 km on horseback during his exploration of the American southwest. In 1683, he discovered that California was not an island, as had been supposed, and in 1701 he mounted an expedition to the Gila and Colorado Rivers. From the nineteenth century onwards, exploration of the American deserts became more intensive. Benjamin Bonneville (1796–1878), John Charles Fremont (1813–90) and Howard Stanbury explored the Great Salt Lake and California respectively.

Central and South America were discovered by the conquistadores. This chapter of the history of discovery was the bloodiest of all. The conquistadores destroyed the great civilizations of the Aztecs, the Incas and the Mayas in their obsessive search for the legendary land and gold of El Dorado. In 1796, Thaddaeus Haenke (1761–1816), a natural scientist from

'Despite the fact that the streets and alleyways of the district we

first entered were so narrow that two riders could scarcely pass

one another, the density of the population and the prosperous

appearance of this part of the city made a great impression on

me. Thus I had at last happily reached the goal of my long

westward journey, the much dreamed-of Timbuktu.'

Heinrich Barth

Bohemia, was sent by the Spanish Crown to explore the Atacama. He was to examine all the flora and fauna, ascertain if they were of any commercial value, and search for mineral resources. Haenke found the deposits of saltpetre in the Atacama, and was able to make explosives and gunpowder with it. He died in mysterious circumstances, probably supporting a rebellion against the Spanish. Haenke has been forgotten in Europe, but in South America he is still talked of in the same breath as Alexander von Humboldt.

In 1939, the German mathematician Maria Reiche (1903–98) heard about strange land markings in Lima: they ran through the Peruvian Coastal Desert, and had been discovered shortly before by the historian Paul Kosok. For fifty years, she studied these so-called Nasca lines, and was able to demonstrate that some of them were connected with astronomical phenomena, and others at their intersections marked the solstices and the seasons.

THE DISCOVERY OF THE AFRICAN DESERTS   The discovery of Africa and of its deserts began many centuries ago. In the third century BC, Alexander the Great penetrated as far as the Siwa Oasis, where he visited the Temple of Amon and was greeted by a priest as the son of Zeus. In 430 BC, Herodotus, the first truly great explorer, wrote about the Garamants in the Libyan Desert, and about five members of the Nasamon tribe who crossed the Sahara and in the south came upon black people as well as a great river. The Romans undertook many expeditions to the Sahara, and penetrated as far as Chad. Ptolemy, the Greek geographer, put together a relatively accurate picture of the Sahara as early as the second century AD, and he identified individual forms of landscape.

In 1352, Ibn Battutah, who had already travelled widely through Arabia and Asia, took a caravan across the Sahara and followed the Niger, which he took to be the Nile, as far as Timbuktu. In the sixteenth century, another great Arab traveller crossed the Sahara: Leo Africanus (c. 1485 – c. 1554) from Cordoba. At the age of sixteen, he accompanied his uncle as part of a Moroccan legation to Timbuktu. Later he made a second journey to Timbuktu, from where he journeyed to Lake Chad and then back through Nubia. After a journey to Egypt, he fell into the hands of pirates off the Tunisian coast, and ended up at the court of Pope Leo X, where he was converted to Christianity. He became a professor of Arabic at Bologna University, and wrote a description of Africa in Italian which was the main source of information about North Africa for a long time.

The turn of the eighteenth/nineteenth century saw the beginning of a systematic exploration of the Sahara. The legendary Timbuktu seemed to exercise an extraordinary power of attraction to Europeans. The German theologian Friedrich Hornemann (1772–1801) left Cairo in September 1798 disguised as a Muslim trader, went first to Siwa, then further west to Murzuk, then to the capital of Fezzan, and from there to Bornu. But he never reached Timbuktu. He died of dysentery on the way. In 1825, the British government sent Major Alexander Gordon Laing (1793–1826) to Africa, with the task of reaching Timbuktu from the north and ascertaining the course of the Niger. He decided to take a caravan route that no European had used before, through Ghadames in present-day Libya, and in August 1926 he reached Timbuktu. From there he went to Segu in order to follow the Niger, but on the way he was murdered by his companions. The Frenchman René Caillié (1799–1838) was luckier. He reached Timbuktu in April 1828, having started from Senegal. Caillié had learned Arabic and posed as the son of Muslim parents from Alexandria. He stayed in Timbuktu for two weeks, in constant danger of being unmasked, but then he joined a caravan that was heading for Morocco across the western Sahara. When he returned to Paris, he was awarded the prize offered by the Geographical Society for the first person to reach Timbuktu.

HEINRICH BARTH  Through the mediation of the Prussian Ambassador to England, Heinrich Barth (1821–65) – a geography lecturer at Berlin University – joined the geologist Adolf Overweg on a British expedition which left Tripoli in 1850 and crossed the Sahara to Bornu. Richardson, the leader of the expedition, died in 1851, but Barth and Overweg went on alone, and explored the whole region around Lake Chad, sometimes together but sometimes separately. In 1852, Overweg died too. Barth headed west, and in 1853 he reached Timbuktu, where he stayed for seven months. On his return journey, he met his compatriot Eduard Vogel, who had been sent to rescue him. In spring 1855, Barth left Bornu, travelled through Bilma and Murzuk, and finally – after an absence of almost six years – arrived home. In the course of this

Heinrich Barth

continuously dangerous expedition, he proved himself to be one of the ablest explorers in the long history of desert exploration. His five-volume report fills 3,593 pages, and is still regarded today as an indispensable source of information on the history of the Sahara.

GERHARD ROHLFS AND GUSTAV NACHTIGAL    Gerhard Rohlfs (1831–96) and Gustav Nachtigal (1834–85) helped to broaden the world's knowledge of the Sahara, although later they were to enter into colonial service. Gerhard Rohlfs was the first European to cross the Sahara (1865–67), and got as far as Lagos. Later, he undertook two major expeditions into the Libyan Desert, and in 1879 he was also the first European to reach the Kufra Oasis. Gustav Nachtigal travelled with a caravan to Murzuk, and from there went on an expedition to the Tibesti highlands, which again he was the first European to reach. In 1873, he succeeded in entering the forbidden kingdom of Wadai.

ALEXINE TINNE    In Murzuk, Nachtigal met Alexine Tinne (1835–69), one of the few women explorers of Africa. She was a rich heiress of Anglo-Dutch descent, and always travelled with a large entourage. In 1869, she set out on an expedition across the Sahara to Murzuk, with the intention of finding out whether there was a watercourse linking Lake Chad and the Nile. From Murzuk she wanted to go through Bornu to the Upper Nile, but while Nachtigal was exploring the Tibesti, Alexine Tinne was being robbed and murdered in Ghat.

THEODORE MONOD    Even at the beginning of the twentieth century, knowledge of the Sahara was still far from complete. After most of it had been conquered and portioned off as part of the French Empire, officers from the camel corps were given the task of exploring it systematically. Later, they were joined by scientists like Théodore Monod, one of the most important Sahara explorers of the twentieth century. He was in fact an oceanographer, but from 1927 onwards undertook countless Saharan expeditions by camel, collecting stones and fossils, discovering the skeleton of a prehistoric man, and studying the flora and fauna. In 1936, he crossed the Tanezrouft desert for the first time, and in 1954 the Majabat-al-Koubra Plateau ('Great Loneliness') in the borderland between Mauritania and Mali.

In 1923, the Egyptian Ahmed Hassanein Bey, accompanied by thirty-seven camels, crossed the Libyan Desert to the Kufra Oasis, and went on to El Fashir in the Sudan. On the way, he dis-

Gustav Nachtigal

covered the long-sought-after oases of Jebel Arkenu and Jebel Uweinat. However, it proved difficult to cross the whole expanse of the Libyan Desert with caravans, and it was not until motorized vehicles and aircraft were available that comprehensive exploration became possible. The Austro-Hungarian motor and aviation pioneer Ladislaus E. Almásy (1865–1951) soon became known as a leading expert on the eastern Sahara. As an officer in Hungary, then allied to Germany, he worked for the German Secret Service in the Second World War, smuggling spies across the desert to Egypt. His story is told in the film *The English Patient*.

With the narrowness of its east-west dimensions, the Namib was never much of an attraction for explorers. Only when it was incorporated into the colony of 'German Southwest Africa' and diamonds were discovered there in 1908 did the researchers suddenly become interested. In 1963, a Desert Research Institute was set up in Gobabeb. The dune massif from the Kuiseb to Lüderitz is still virtually inaccessible even today, as it lies in the Namib Naukluft National Park and the no-go area of the diamond mines.

Most of the world's deserts have now been 'discovered', but travellers may still find large areas that are fascinating to explore and have had few human visitors. Travel today, however, is not necessarily any less dangerous than it used to be. Modern satellite navigation, comprehensive maps, and reliable modes of transport certainly help to prevent people from getting lost and dying of thirst, but landmines, bandits, rebels, terrorists and drug smugglers ensure that travelling in many Asian and African deserts remains unpredictable.

Desert exploration today is as multifaceted as science itself. Many branches of the natural sciences are concerned with matters unique to the desert, and their specialized approach brings new knowledge. Geography, for instance, can help to organize and evaluate findings spatially, but nowadays much of the data is acquired in the laboratory or by way of satellites. Such long-distance observations are crucial for the study of desert climates. The evolution of desert climates is inextricably bound up with that of the world's climate in general. Floods, droughts and storms have become an increasing danger. The industrialized nations are also beginning to realize that the extremes brought about by climate change not only have terrible ecological consequences, but can also do incalculable damage economically and socially.

The slopes are steep. Man and beast struggle onwards. Again and again we have to use our hands to shovel the sand aside, to smooth out the sharp ridges of the dunes and open a path for the caravan. The camels hang back at the difficulty, and then fall down. In order to make this charming story even more exciting, our guides now inform us that we have most certainly missed the well.... It all sounds very promising.'

Théodore Monod

# DESERT EXPLORATION FROM SPACE

## PROFESSOR DR STEFAN DECH

When astronauts look down on Planet Earth from a height of 300 km, and report back on the most impressive sights they see, the first thing they mention is usually the deserts. Why? Above all, it is the absence of human beings. The landscapes that most of us see day after day consist of buildings and streets, or maybe farms and forests. Deserts are the exact opposite of what we are used to – uncultivated, untouched, pure nature.

The most significant aspect of their surface is the almost complete lack of vegetation. The bare elements of texture, structure and form are therefore clearly visible, since there is neither plant nor concrete to mask them. The smallest differences in the character and the mineral composition of the surface are immediately evident in satellite photographs, and when the sun is low, the shadows give the landscape a strangely sculptured appearance.

Long-distance exploration provides detailed measurements and data about land and ice surfaces, oceans and the atmosphere without any direct contact with what is being explored. The bearer of the data is reflected or emitted light, or electromagnetic rays. Every object and every surface under observation delivers its own spectral fingerprints, and these will vary according to conditions and the time of day. The 'spectral' data, which can be in the form of satellite pictures, then serve geographers as a basis of information and analysis which for many years now has been essential for geomorphological and geological mapping. It is now unthinkable for any expedition to set forth without the aid of satellite maps. Of increasing importance is the gathering of precise data concerning geophysical and biophysical statistics such as the albedo (the fraction of incident light reflected by an object), surface temperatures, and the emissions, coverage and biomass of plants. Digital cameras and radiometers operate 'passively', recording radiation in the optical spectral field. 'Active' instruments such as radar

In 1972, with the first of the American Landsat satellites, there began a new era in the exploration of the Earth. By staying on the same orbit, the Landsat can take pictures of the entire surface of the Earth as it rotates.

Sand and rock formations near Terkezi in Chad.

Satellite picture from 700 km up.

sensors irradiate the Earth's surface with microwaves and then record the echoes sent back by the objects targeted. This technique has several advantages: radar instruments do not depend on the time of day or night, because they 'illuminate' the Earth themselves. The waves can penetrate clouds and trace gases and materials virtually unhindered, and so they can supply data regardless of weather conditions. If radar echoes are used to evaluate one and the same object from slightly different angles, one can build up digital models of the landscape (in which even individual dunes can be distinguished) and capture the tiniest shifts in the Earth's surface. This process can be used to predict the future, as it can analyse what is happening or is likely to happen in potential earthquake or volcanic regions, mass movements, and cave-ins after the extraction of gas or groundwater. It can even deliver information about events below the Earth's surface: microwaves can actually penetrate a few centimetres into the ground.

Let us now consider some of the advantages to be gained by long-distance exploration of deserts. First of all, long-distance sensors can deliver data about everything on the surface – in contrast to all terrestrial information-gathering techniques, no matter how many observation posts there might be. This is the biggest advantage of all, particularly in remote desert regions or those that are inaccessible for political reasons. Such methods will become increasingly important in the future for exploring large areas and observing their development. Then there are the technical advantages: there are various qualities of dissolution according to the type of sensor and the constellation of satellites. For instance, definition (spatial dissolution) – the sharpness with which an image is reproduced – has become amazingly sophisticated. Civil satellite sensors today generally have dissolutions of up to 60 cm edge-length per pixel (the smallest measuring unit in satellite data, derived from 'picture element'), but for cartography on an average scale of 1:200,000, systems are used with pixel dissolution of 10–30 m. The more detailed the spatial dissolution of the data, the smaller the area per photograph will be, owing to the quantity of data to be captured. A photograph from the Landsat type of satellite will cover some 200 km.

In addition to enhanced recognition of objects, the classification of surfaces and their mineral or vegetable contents is an important facet of exploration from space. Here it is a

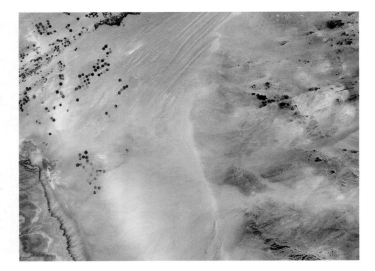

From the Russian space station MIR, 250 km up, one can make out the circular irrigation zones in the Rub al-Khali.

362

Satellite picture, taken from 700 km up, of the Namib dunes split by the Tsauchab.

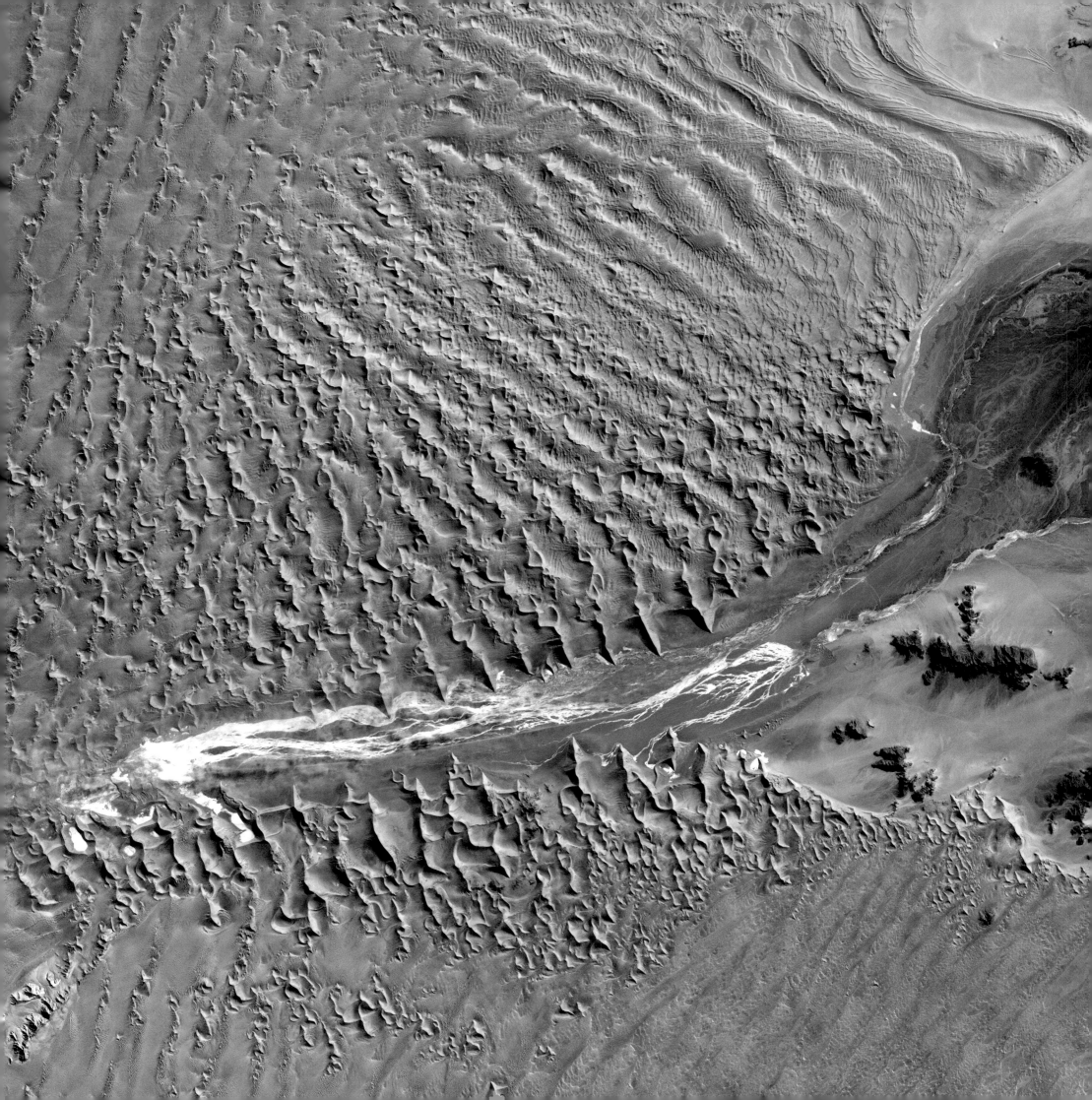

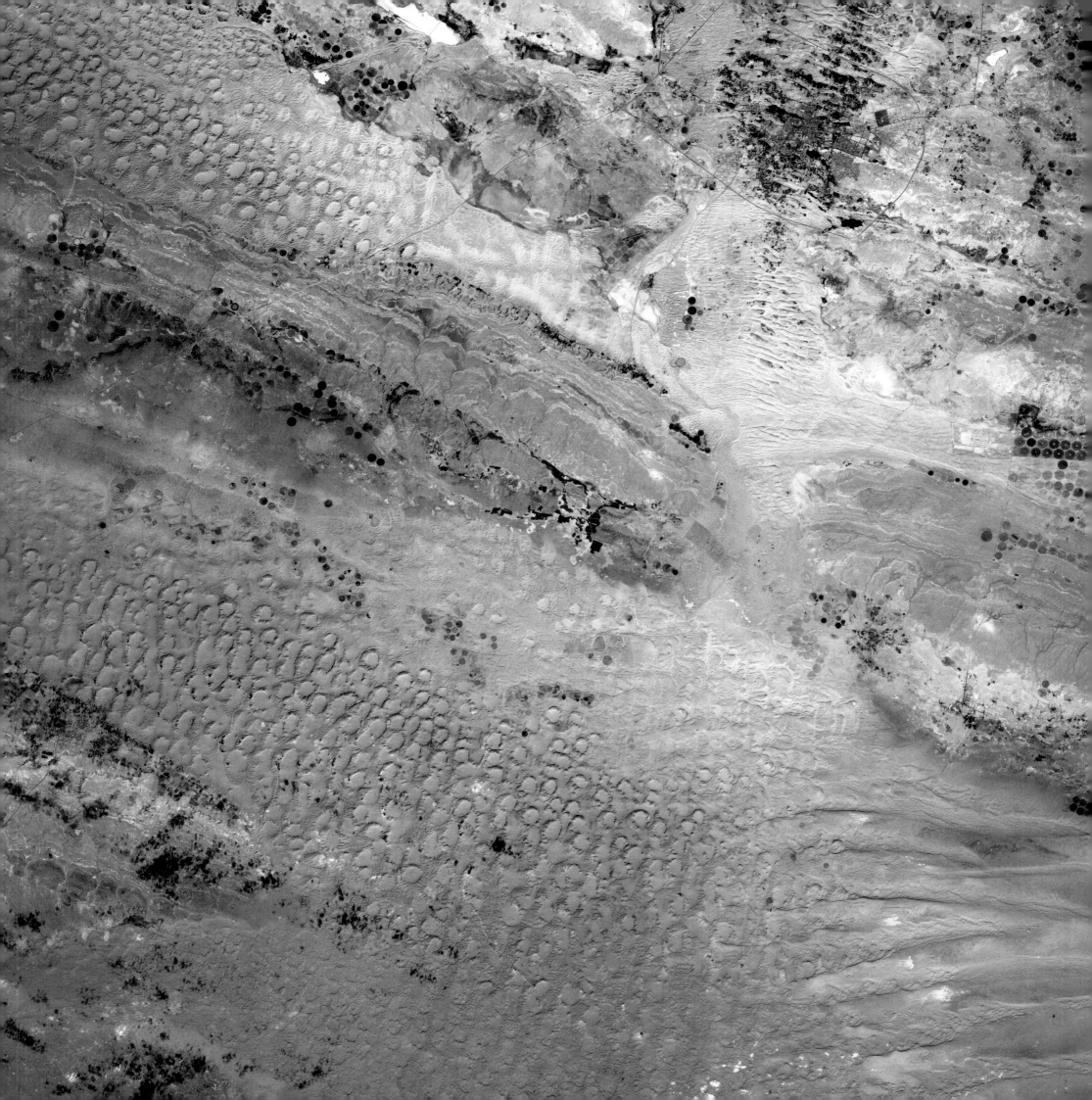

matter of the 'spectral' dissolution of long-distance data-gathering. This is defined by the measured section of the electromagnetic spectrum and the precision with which differentiations can be made within it. With greater spatial and spectral dissolution, one can determine not only the type of desert surface (e.g. serir, hammada, erg), but also the mineral composition (the proportion of limestone, salt, iron, manganese etc.). In the limestone crusts, for instance, there are enormous quantities of carbon, and these are potentially of major importance in changing climatic conditions. If rainfall were to increase, considerable amounts of this trapped carbon from early geosynclines (sedimentary deposits) could be released, thereby further raising the $CO_2$ content of the atmosphere.

As regards farming and other forms of cultivation, which are hindered by salinization or desertification, once again long-distance surveys can be of great help, as can be seen from the example of the Aral Sea. Situated in semi-arid Central Asia, the Aral Sea has been drying up on a dramatic scale since 1960. It was once the fourth largest inland sea in the world, but as a result of intensive irrigation measures along its inlets, the rivers Amur Darya and Syr Darya, the hydrological balance has been destroyed. The consequences, described in the chapters on 'The Deserts of Central Asia', have been devastating both for the people and for the environment. In order to improve this catastrophic economic and ecological situation, data is being collected over the whole region. The aim is to build up an information system that will eventually serve as a basis for regeneration through sustainable exploitation. The results will also be applicable to other semi-arid regions with similar problems. Long-distance data-gathering is being used for the following tasks: to document the drying-up process and the volume of water that remains; to identify and monitor processes of degradation such as erosion and soil salinization; to register climatological parameters (temperature, evaporation); to monitor exploitation of the land and the changes that it causes; to record deterioration of surfaces and seasonal cycles of useful vegetation; to optimize use of water and to determine the best times for irrigation. All this data will be made available to experts and to local inhabitants, and the conclusions will then be put to practical use. Satellite pictures may offer us an impressive view but they are also playing an increasingly important role in the practical aspects of desert research.

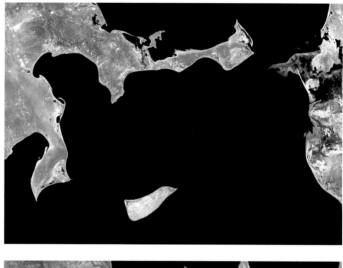

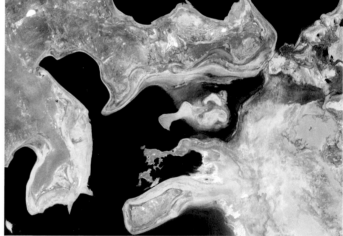

**Top:** Northeastern part of the Aral Sea in 1973, taken from 700 km up.

**Bottom:** This satellite picture of 2000 clearly shows how the Aral Sea has dried up.

Satellite picture, from 300 km up, of extensive star-dunes east of Buraydah, Saudi Arabia.

# DESERTS OF THE EARTH — OUT AND ABOUT

Michael at the erg of Admer, Algeria

Aïr, Niger

Michael with daughter Gina in Aïr

Morning light, Tassili du Hoggar, Algeria

In front of the Himalayas, Tibet

Elke with her film camera

Stuck at Salar de Uyuni, Bolivia

Pleased by the good evening light

Winter's evening on the Altiplano

Daughters Gina and Rita, Namibia

Breakfast on the Atacama

Hotel in Tibet

This book is based on a long journey through the deserts of the Earth. My friend Elke and I travelled together across five continents and more than fifty countries on a BMW R1150 GS motorcycle. Our journey began and ended in Munich, and lasted 900 days, split up over several stages through a period of five years. The maximum range of our motorcycle was 700 km, thanks to some special equipment, and we always carried enough food and water for a few days. Most of our space was taken up by film and camera equipment and materials. We nearly always slept out in the open air, and cooked on a tiny kerosene stove. As we tended to follow the winter, because the desert light is clearer then and there is less need for water, the cold often gave us more trouble than the heat. Obtaining visas and the necessary papers required endless patience. Some countries do not give visas to individual travellers, while China forbids entry with a vehicle. At various points there was also a threat to our own personal safety. The uncomplicated journeys to Australia and Chile, on the other hand, were a real treat. Generally, our travel plans centred on seeing the focal points of the landscape, meeting all our logistical needs, and looking after our own safety. Where and when the day would end – it usually began before dawn – was something we could very rarely determine in advance. One decisive factor was the light, which had to be bright and clear for the photographs, but was sometimes totally lacking. In such cases, we had to go back to the same place, often more than once, until we felt that we had taken the photographs we wanted.

Michael Martin, April 2004, Munich

Overnight at Salar de Uyuni

Elke with Rajasthanis, India

Laguna Verde, Bolivia

Arakao, Niger

# BIOGRAPHIES

MICHAEL MARTIN  Photographer and author Michael Martin is a specialist in deserts. He was born in Munich in 1963, and at the age of seventeen had already developed a passion for deserts. Over the next twenty years, he undertook eighty expeditions across the deserts of Africa, published fifteen illustrated books, and gave more than one thousand lectures in the German-speaking world. In 1999, he decided that his next subject would be the deserts of the Earth. During the five years that followed, he and his partner Elke Wallner crossed every desert in every continent, travelling through over fifty countries.

Michael Martin studied geography, ethnology and politics in Munich, and has a degree in geography. He is an outstanding desert photographer and equally brilliant lecturer, whose talks have inspired hundreds of thousands of people in many different countries. His books and lectures have won a large number of awards, and the former have sold many thousands of copies (for further information about his work, lectures, workshops and exhibitions, log onto www.photographermichaelmartin.com). He and his family live in Munich.

MICHAEL ASHER  Michael Asher was the first European to cross the Sahara from west to east – a journey of more than 7,000 km on foot and by camel. His desert expeditions have won awards from the Royal Geographical Society, and many of his books – including those on Lawrence of Arabia, Wilfred Thesiger and the Sahara – have been bestsellers.

KLAUS GIESSNER  Professor Dr Klaus Giessner: 1964–68 compiler of African map book; 1975–84 Professor and Head of African Department at the Geographical Institute of Würzburg University; since 1984, Chair of Physical Geography at the Catholic University of Eichstätt-Ingolstadt. He was made emeritus professor in 2003.

ULRICH WERNERY  Dr Ulrich Wernery is a veterinary surgeon specializing in tropical animal diseases; since 1987 he has been Science Director of the Central Research Laboratory in Dubai, and part-time lecturer at Munich University.

STEFAN DECH  Professor Dr Stefan Dech is Director of the DLR (the German Aerospace Center), and has held the Chair of Long Range Exploration at Würzburg University since 2001.

# ACKNOWLEDGMENTS

## GERMANY

Yvonne Meyer-Lohr, who designed this book and made a major contribution to the overall concept. Her creativeness and professionalism, as well as her enthusiasm and her total commitment to the project, have played a large part in the making of this book.

Petra Soelzer for her assistance in the design.

Dieter Kirchner and his team from Novaconcept, Berlin, for their unique lithography and for personal commitment to this project.

Gudrun Honke, editor, for her patience, commitment and extraordinary efficiency.

Karlheinz Rau, production manager, and his colleague Stefanie Baiter, for their commitment, calm and competence.

Robert Meisner, Nils Sparwasser and Bernhard Schnüriger for the immense amount of trouble they took in compiling the maps.

Monika Thaler and Gert Frederking, publishers, for their courage in supporting such a massive, long-term project. From the very start, they believed in it, had faith in me, and gave me the freedom to translate my ideas into reality.

Ute Heek, senior editor of the Frederking & Thaler Verlag, who supported and was personally involved in this project from the beginning.

Angela Kesselring, Tanja Warter, Regina Wiesmaier and Eva Clausen, members of the publishing team, for all their help.

The printers at the Druckerei Passavia, Passau.

Leica for their perfect cameras and lens. I should like in particular to thank Hanns-Peter Cohn, Gero Furchheim, Michael Agel, Oliver Richter, Bernd Henrichs, Tina Wiesner and Ralf Hagenauer.

BMW for their wonderfully reliable motorcycle, a BMW R 1150 GS, which never let us down. My special thanks to Christoph von Tschirrschnitz, Herrn Geisenhofer, Herrn Kugler, Herrn Carl and the workshop team at the Motor Cycle Centre in Munich.

Serac for providing the perfect clothing for both heat and cold. My personal thanks to Thomas Brunner, Heinz Brunner, Andrea Stetter, Thomas Schumacher and Michael Böhm.

Travel Overland for their help in arranging our countless flights.

Particular thanks to Isabell Nehring and Peter Glandien and the Travel Overland team at Munich Airport, especially Gabi Bachmaier.

Professors Jäkel and Hofmann for their invaluable advice concerning the Ala Shan desert; Dr Wernery, Professor Giessner and Professor Dech, whose special contributions are an enrichment of this book; Dr Robert Meisner of the DLR, who supplied the satellite maps.

Stefan Bässgen of Bässgen AV-Technik, whose inventiveness and personal commitment have been vital ingredients of my lectures and slide presentations over the last twenty years.

Peida Defilla von Boa, whose company BOA Videofilmkunst was involved in our film project from the very beginning.

Erich Hochmeyer and Jacques Steinhauser of Prismachrome, Munich, for their ever reliable service in developing my films.

Herbert Schwarz and Jochen Schanz of Touratech, whose products were of great assistance on our motorcycle rides across the deserts.

Günter Tröber, my tax consultant, for many years of good advice.

Our friends and colleagues Bernhard Edmaier, Angelika Jung-Hütti, Norbert and Eli Rosing, Heinz and Angelika Zak, Hartmut and Eli Krinitz, Holger Fritzsche and Sylvia Kreller, Karl Johaentges and Jackie Blackwood, Roland Adams, Gerhard Göttler, with all of whom we often discussed this project.

Alex Schwindt from Art of Vision, who is responsible for the programming of my website and my slide shows.

Sylvia and Rainer Jarosch of Suntours, who are among the greatest experts on the Sahara; Julietta Baums of Nomad Reisen, who is an expert on Arabian countries; Nils Hallenberg of Active Tours, who arranged our motorcycle entry into China.

Christoph Hofbauer and Klaus Hledik, of Druckmedien, Munich, for whose friendly advice and printing know-how I am extremely grateful.

My colleagues Tine Wittmann, Thilo Mössner, Dorothea Büchele and Wojo Kavcic for their loyalty and their commitment.

My parents Gerda and Gerhard Martin for their open-mindedness and their support for all my plans and ideas.

Paula Schermer, Gerda and Gerhard Martin, Eli and Michel Bloss, Steffi and Bernd Wittmann, Marlene Lochbrunner for looking after our children during our many expeditions.

Our children Gina, David, Nathalie, Rita and Antonia, who tried to cause as little trouble as possible while we were away, and who often accompanied us.

My greatest thanks go to my friend and travelling companion Elke Wallner for her love, her support and her commitment.

## AFGHANISTAN

Saleem Faige for being our interpreter and for providing us with so many insights into Afghan society. Hermann Ester for his morning espressos in Kabul. Lajos for his optimism, without which we would never have gone to Afghanistan. The International Red Cross for their hospitality in Bamiyan.

## ALGERIA

Cheikh Meliakh from Adrar Bous, Tamanrasset, for organizing the different stages of our journey through Algeria; our guide Bashir from Djanet for his help in crossing the Tassili du Hoggar.

## AUSTRALIA

Randall for our days at Anna Creek. Keryl Evans for our visit to her farm. The Australian Aboriginal leader Yami Lester for a revealing conversation. Linsey and Anne Mathews for the flight and for their hospitality. Al Lad and his family for information about opal mining.

## BURKINA FASO

Sebastian Seitz for his hospitality in Ouagadougou.

## CHAD

Omar and Hassan for their help in repairing our front tyre and for safely guiding us through the minefields.

## CHINA

Liu Wen Hua for organizing our motorcycle ride through China and Tibet. Mirkamil and Jasmin for accompanying us through the Chinese deserts. Dawa for accompanying us to the sacred mountain of Kailash.

## IRAN

Ali for accompanying us with such endless patience.

## MONGOLIA

Nara for accompanying us through Mongolia. Helge Reitz of Nomads Adventure for her excellent organization of our journey.

## NAMIBIA

Thomas Bauer and Christine Schmid for our Ultra Light flights. Mousse von Solitaire for a long friendship, and the Grönning family for many years of support.

## NIGER

Ahmed Ewaden, head of Ewaden Voyages, Agadez, for organizing the different stages of our journey through Niger.

## OMAN

Miguel for his good advice. Rashid for his hospitality among the dunes of Ramlat al Wahiba.

## QATAR

Abdulhalim Albader for organizing our stay. Khalifa Al-Baidly for inviting us to a workshop and lecture in Qatar. Sheikh Soud for inviting us to his country.

## TURKMENISTAN

Oleg, Flat and Valera for their stamina in crossing the Kara Kum.

## UAE

Renate and Uli Wernery for their warm welcome in Dubai and for important contacts. Andres Pohl for letting us attend the training of the royal falcons. Eli and Martin Nutz for their hospitality in Abu Dhabi. Mia Hedman for giving us insight into the world of the luxury hotel Burj el Arab. Sheikh Seid for showing us his falcons.

## USA

Thomas Herz and Bernhard von Thaden for taking care of our motorcycle.

## YEMEN

Mohamed Ali, for invaluable assistance through his many contacts.

# INDEX

## INDEX OF PEOPLE

The 18 satellite maps were supplied by the German Remote Sensing Data Center of DLR, Oberpfaffenhofen.
The maps are based on data of the MODIS-Sensor provided by NASA-GSFC.

Satellite Images
Page 360: Landsat-7, taken from 700 km up on 22.10.2000. Source: USGS EROS Data Center, Sioux Falls, SD, USA.
Page 362: MOMS, taken from 250 km up on 18.12.1996. Source: DLR – the German Aerospace Center, Oberpfaffenhofen.
Page 363: Landsat-7, taken from 700 km up on 12.8.2000. Source: USGS EROS Data Center, Sioux Falls, SD, USA.
Page 364: MOMS, taken from 250 km up. Source: DLR – the German Aerospace Center, Oberpfaffenhofen.
Page 365: Landsat-7, taken from 700 km up on 29.5.1973 and 29.7.2000. Source: USGS EROS Data Center, Sioux Falls, SD, USA.

Historical Pictures
The pictures on pages 350 and 357 were kindly supplied by the Heinrich-Barth-Institut, Cologne.
The picture on page 353 was kindly supplied by the National Museum of Ethnography, Stockholm.
The picture on page 358 was kindly supplied by the the town of Stendal, the birthplace of Gustav Nachtigal.

4: Tassili du Hoggar, Algeria, Africa
7: Arakao, Niger, Africa
26–27: Monastery in the Ala Shan desert, Asia
130–131: The Gibson desert, Australia
160–161: Paria Plateau, USA
218–219: Tassili du Hoggar, Algeria, Africa
302–303: Tassili du Hoggar, Algeria, Africa

Scholarly Contributions By:
Professor Dr Giessner, Chair of Physical Geography, Katholische Universität Eichstätt–Ingolstadt
'Changes in the Saharan Desert and Landscape', pages 317–321
Dr Wernery, Ludwig-Maximilians-Universität, Munich
'The Camel and the Desert', pages 337–341
Professor Dr Dech, DLR – the German Aerospace Center, Oberpfaffenhofen
'Desert Exploration from Space', pages 361–365

Typography, Design and Setting: Yvonne Meyer-Lohr and Petra Soeltzer, Kommunikationsdesign, Düsseldorf
Reproduction: NovaConcept Kirchner GmbH, Berlin
Printing and Binding: Passavia Druckservice GmbH, Passau
Paper: BVS matt made by Scheufelen, Lenningen

First published in the United Kingdom in 2004 by Thames & Hudson Ltd, 181A High Holborn, London WC1V 7QX

www.thamesandhudson.com

English translation from the German *Die Wüsten der Erde* by David H. Wilson

British Library Cataloguing-in-Publication Data
A catalogue record for this book is available from the British Library

ISBN 0-500-51194-2

Printed and bound in Germany